"Viola Neufeld breaks vital new ground in how to embrace conflict and reveal its hidden gifts. She walks us through the process patiently, gently. Along the way we become able to relax, breathe, heal and grow in ways we never thought possible. We come to realize, with wonder, that the transformations we seek actually *require* conflict. And that changes everything. I'd say that you need this book, but it's more accurate to say that the world needs this book!"

—*Raphael Cushnir,*
author of *The One Thing Holding You Back*

"Most of us struggle with conflict in one form or another, be it internal or external. *Grateful for the Fight* is a journey in self-awareness that provides perspectives to understand why we fear conflict, and tools to approach it with curiosity. Viola Neufeld has 30 years of experience in this field. Trust that there is value in this process and you will never approach conflict in the same way again. I wish I had read this book 20 years ago."

—*Kathy Troupe,*
Executive Director, ACETECH

"Once in a long while, a book that can change our important relationships comes around. *Grateful for the Fight* is one such book. Conflict is both human and inevitable. The question is, how does one respond to conflict in a healing, redemptive, and a relationship-preserving way? Viola's book is informative, cogent, and perceptive. A seasoned counselor for decades, Viola guides the reader through the maze of understanding, engaging, and changing our approaches to conflict. We have read no better handbook for anyone who hopes to transcend old habits of conflict and yearns for a more successful and life-giving map."

—*Dr. Thomas Cooper / Dr. Karen Cooper,*
Founder of City in Focus /Author

"Much more than an informative read, *Grateful for the Fight* entices us into a journey of personal transformation. In her engaging, practical and vulnerable style, Viola Neufeld challenges us to harness the hidden value of conflict with others as a pathway to see and grow from our inner conflict. This book is relevant, powerful and life-changing."

—*Peter Mogan*
Partner Mogan Daniel Slager LLP

"The message of this book is surprising. Don't waste your fights! Instead, be grateful for them. Viola Neufeld thinks that our external conflicts provide rich insight into our internal conflicts—a source of our fighting. Full of practical, clinical wisdom from a seasoned couple's therapist. I highly recommend this book."

—*M. Wesley Buch*,
Ph.D., Registered Psychologist, Behavioural Health Care

Undeniably the most comprehensive book ever written that leads you to easily understand why that horrible pointed finger *must* turn back toward you! Viola Neufeld turns complex psychological theory into interesting, relatable prose that keep you reading. Viola brings a new slant to the word opportunity by providing us with a way to get "unstuck" that brings freedom to ourselves and the conflict we're imprisoned by. This book brings you out on the other side more whole than you went in."

—*Ingrid Kandal*
President, CEO, BC Health Services Ltd.

GRATEFUL
FOR THE FIGHT

Using inner conflict to
transform yourself and
your relationships

Viola Neufeld

 FriesenPress

Suite 300 - 990 Fort St
Victoria, BC, V8V 3K2
Canada

www.friesenpress.com

ISBN
978-1-5255-1406-7 (Hardcover)
978-1-5255-1407-4 (Paperback)
978-1-5255-1408-1 (eBook)

1. SELF-HELP, COMMUNICATION & SOCIAL SKILLS

Distributed to the trade by The Ingram Book Company

Dedicated to Diet

Jor, Jess, Jem and Josh

Acknowledgements

My first word of thanks goes to my remarkable business partner, John Radford, who has generously assisted me on this long writing journey. His substantial input in this material, my work, and my life, is invaluable. He has shaped my thinking as we've collaborated with our clients to find a way through their conflict. This book wouldn't have come to completion the way it has without John.

I am deeply grateful to my clients for the privilege of entering their sacred space. This is deeply personal work, never to be taken lightly. As they have courageously addressed themselves and their challenging relationships, they have encouraged me to do the same. Their lives have inspired me, and the conversations have profoundly enriched my life. Thank you.

Naomi Pauls, editor at Paper Trail Publishing, worked painstakingly and generously on an early draft. Marian Sandmaier, Writer and Book Editor, gave me wings in her encouraging developmental edit and made me smile with her many key suggestions. Trena White of Page Two Strategies served as a supportive coach, and Kendra Ward, their editor, made the material move by reducing words and choosing active ones in a copy line edit. I am appreciative beyond words for editors who clarify and refine the writing. Working with Heather Symes around the graphics reminded me on each encounter that there are good people everywhere. Thank you to Jamie Ollivier, Emma Pickering, and Teresita Hernandez-Quesada at FriesenPress for assisting me through the publishing process. Many thanks to friends who offered extensive feedback on the various versions of the manuscript: their questions and recommendations improved the rendering significantly.

And I am incredibly grateful to my family—the most intimate of relationships—where working through conflict can be the most difficult and most rewarding. Each of our four children has forced me to face myself and given me the opportunity to grow. Thank you for investing candidly and compassionately in our relationship.

Then there is my dear husband, Diet, who has been my life's companion in learning about conflict, intimacy and love. I am so grateful to him for hanging in during difficult conversations, for caring about how his behavior affected me, for helping me see how my behavior was affecting him, for offering perspective when I was losing mine, for making me laugh amid the trouble, for never losing his ability to delight in life, and for loving me bigheartedly. Diet passed away recently. This material was written before he died, but was not yet in publishable form. My deepest gratitude goes to Diet for every stimulating, challenging, and comforting conversation. A highpoint of every day was coming home to him.

Table of Contents

Introduction

Significant conflict with others invites us on an intensely personal journey. Do we accept the invitation or not? Intuitively we know that conflict asks us to dig deeper within ourselves than we have dug before, to hang in there longer than we think we can during a difficult situation, and to go further than we can see ahead to achieve a breakthrough. Sorting through the inner turmoil of relationship difficulty is never simple, quick, or easy. We can be realistic about the challenges and uncertainties ahead, yet if we forgo the journey through the conflict, the tension remains.

Would it make any difference if you knew that the conflict journey would offer considerable internal peace, even if your opponent doesn't take part? *Grateful for the Fight* stems from my thirty-plus years of helping individuals, couples, families, and organizations navigate conflict. When they're stuck in one spot or feeling as if they are going around in circles, I help clients find a way to move on. Rather than simply managing the challenging relationship better, I encourage clients to use conflict as a valuable window into the self: because it points to our own internal struggle, conflict with others not only helps us get to know ourselves better, but also helps us deal with what keeps us stuck. When we push through that which holds us back, we set ourselves free to be what we can and want to be.

A Transformational Approach

Because of the immense discomfort it triggers, we often run from conflict. Sometimes we create elaborate strategies to avoid conflict at all costs. The approach I offer here is to view conflict as an ally that helps us plumb the depths of ourselves in the interest of achieving personal transformation and, when possible, harmony in our relationships. This is not meaningless mining, then, but purposeful exploration during which we go within to come out differently. Conflict provides us with one of the most direct opportunities to really see who we are and who the other is.

This book shows you how to use external conflict to work through internal conflict and, conversely, how you can use the internal fight to work through the external one. Each relies on the other. As it happens, we are selectively attracted to the significant fights for us—the ones that undo us—which is why we try to run from them. They activate a sensitive, restless part of our identity that cries for attention. Engaging with "the other" takes us where we would not go on our own; it makes us face our "unwanted self." The premise of *Grateful for the Fight* is that if we have the *necessary* fight with ourselves, we won't have unnecessary fights with others.

This is not a simple process. Some have called it a revolutionary approach, because working through conflict in this manner leads people to transform themselves and their relationships.

Typical approaches to conflict emphasize the importance of containing reactivity and maintaining good conduct amid heightened emotion. In the approach explored in this book, the reactivity itself illuminates our invisible inner landscape—the place where we hide our deepest fears. We are prompted to go inside, to explore our fears and sensitivities, to reveal our inner dialogue, and to confront our self-doubt. By dealing with and embracing our unwanted self, we experience release from many unnecessary forms of conflict.

How This Book Can Help You

You can't simply read this book to achieve the change you desire. Success comes first through self-reflection and then in "working the conflict" by applying this book's proposed principles, concepts, and questions when you're stuck in a situation. You might discover some previously hidden drivers for your behavior. You might begin to view the other's behavior through a kaleidoscope of sorts. You might double back to rethink an assumption rather than settle for a premature conclusion. You might expand the way you think about identity, both your own and another's, until neither seems as straightforward as it once did.

Addressing the complexities of difficult relationships is perplexing even to the sharpest mind. This book is an attempt to give some shape to a process that's not definitive. Rather than focusing on reaching an endpoint, *Grateful for the Fight* aims to help you while you are caught up in conflict, since the outcome of a fight is always uncertain. Conflict is like riding a huge roller coaster for the first time with your eyes closed. You have no idea where the twists and turns will be, when your stomach will be in your throat, or exactly when the ride will end. Whether you're experiencing conflict in an intimate relationship, in a work situation, or with members of your family, this book will highlight matters to look out for, provide signposts, and offer glimmers of hope and light to help you find your way.

You'll see that I ask a lot of questions. I do this precisely because answers are so unclear. Questions are powerful because they open shutters, casting new light on what was previously unseen. Looking out beyond your immediate view reveals the endlessly changing sky. When you think about it, answers are often anticlimactic because they reduce your field of view and decrease your options. My hope is that as you fully engage with the questions, you will find a response for the moment, one that will help you inch forward. And then, perhaps, the questions will lead to other enlightening questions.

The danger here is that, in attempting to make highly complex issues understandable and manageable, this book may appear to simplify issues that have no easy answers. But if the answers were straightforward, you would have figured them out a long time ago. So, to be clear, this is not a how-to book telling you to do this or that and everything will be fine. It is not intended to be formulaic, because life is not like that. *Grateful for the Fight* provides a general orientation; after that, as you explore, discover, and experiment in your own conflict world, the adventure is up to you.

In a regular coaching situation, I would lead by following you. I'm quite aware that trying to help you navigate your way through conflict is a rather strange project to take on in a book. Without your shaping or directing the conversation, I run the risk of speaking beside the points that are relevant to your question or dilemma. But let's attempt to take a journey together. If the ideas and questions I offer resonate with you, you will likely take them in a direction I couldn't have anticipated. You will make connections that are personal to you. What this book offers, then, is not a cookie-cutter approach, but rather the raw ingredients to help you shape answers for your unique situation.

Approaching this work as a journey best mirrors an experience of the conflict process. In the pages that follow, you will read scenarios that reflect real conflict situations, but please be assured that the privacy of all individuals has been protected. If at times you see yourself in the material, then know that you are not alone. When it comes to matters at the core, we are often alike.

Please read this book in any way you'd like—sequentially or by dipping into the sections that hold most appeal. I wrote it to help people get "unstuck," and since this is a lifelong journey, I hope you will return to it whenever you need support during conflict, to remind yourself to go within.

To understand the process outlined in this book, you might find it helpful to visualize an inverted bell curve. Part 1, situated at the top-left of the curve, introduces a helpful way to think about conflict—because if you believe that there's purpose in discomfort (for example, to find a way to increase peace and have a better relationship), you will also be hopeful in the process. This part also advocates using the mind as a tool to deal with our built-in "brain traps." Part 2 begins where you may be now: inadvertently maintaining the fight. It introduces the notion of using the fight to explore inner restlessness. Part 3, at the bottom of the curve, descends deeper into the internal fight to deal with what I call the "unwanted self," and helps you lovingly embrace a fuller self. Part 4 applies your inner fight to six scenarios and helps you discover the value of the fight within. In doing so, both you and "the other," who has triggered your inner conflict, benefit. Part 5 details engaging with the other differently, regardless of what they're doing, because once you have made changes within, the fight must change. You come out from within, ascending the bell curve on the other side, to engage conflict and relationship differently. The book ends with an invitation to let conflict change you, and your future.

THE CONFLICT PROCESS

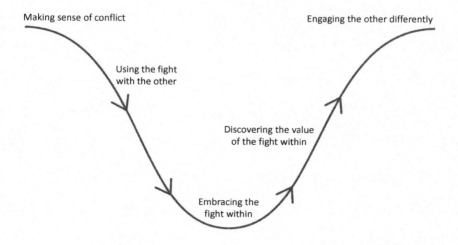

I have taken this journey with hundreds of clients. For more than thirty years, I have heard repeated similar words, witnessed familiar patterns, and observed how people get stuck when conflict activates an identity struggle. I have been privileged to be present as clients tread their sacred ground and make surprising discoveries. Satisfaction comes from watching them push past their limitations and become capable of more than they knew. This is a breakthrough I wish for everyone who experiences conflict—so let's get started.

PART 1
MAKING SENSE OF CONFLICT

At some level, all conflict makes sense, and when we find this level, conflict transforms. But then it becomes something more difficult to face.

CHAPTER 1

Conflict—the Great Attractor

The experience of conflict is everything we don't want, but it might be exactly what we need for healing our sensitivities, growing personally, and making a change. Facing conflict with another is an opportunity to be introspective, which then increases our self-awareness and gives us clarity in *necessary* fights with the other. When we understand ourselves more, we also cast a gentler, kinder eye toward the other.

Many of us have a person who puts us on edge: what they think about us impacts our life in some significant way, and so the relationship is challenging. In this book, I call that person "the other," which is a term used in both philosophy and psychology. Sometimes we're not even in an actual fight, but the strain between us and the possibility of conflict eats away at our sense of contentment. Thinking about a fight might be even more stressful than the actuality of one. Strangely, even against our will, we are drawn to relationships that activate familiar conflicts within us. Much of the strife in our lives drops away almost unnoticeably with the passing of time. But other conflict sticks to us like Velcro. We get reactive around it and it keeps us awake at night. That's the conflict we're attracted to.

Let's now consider the seductive power of conflict, the reasons why we fight, and the value to be gained from embracing conflict.

Attracted to the Fight between and Within

We don't waste time on useless conflict. It sticks only when there's something valuable in it for us, because the fight *between* and the fight *within* are connected. Hence, if we can engage this significant conflict differently, we might be grateful for the fight down the road.

What does our significant conflict look like and how does it work? Let's look at some examples:

- Pradeep's manager ends a congenial conversation by saying, "I'll be out of town for the rest of the week and I hope you'll be productive." As Pradeep walks away, he mutters some obscenities about his ruthless, hard-hearted boss, who's interested only in the bottom line. The word *productive* rings in his ears.

- Ursula is the last one into the car, because she checked and double-checked to make sure the family left the house in order and has everything required for the trip ahead. Feeling on edge, she comments on her children's dreadful music and complains about the messy car. The tension between her and her family members is nothing new. Her teenager says, "Chill … Ease up, Mom. We're on vacation." Ursula wants to yell back but holds her tongue and whispers in her head, "Go to hell … All of you, go to hell." For the rest of the day, the words *ease up* pulsate painfully into a migraine.

- Ike's wife leaves him and he hears from others that she's partying with old friends and new. Ike phones a mutual woman friend who's well-connected in their social circle, and says, "I think my wife is cheating with the husband of someone on your ball team." He believes there must be some explanation for why his wife would leave him. Ike has never thought of himself as a vindictive guy, but now he finds himself ruminating on how he can hurt her back. Previously, Ike had prided himself on being an easygoing, fun-loving, and generous guy.

In these three scenarios, the individual couldn't let the words go because they hit in an area where each struggled with a sense of self. Pradeep got stuck on *productive*. He didn't want to be thought of as unproductive. Ursula fixated on *ease up* because she didn't want to be thought of as uptight. Ike was hooked because his wife did not seem to miss him or be hurting, and that was a blow to his pride. He didn't want to be laughed at by his friends. He wanted to feel important.

The challenge to identity comes in many forms. It might be words spoken or unspoken, deeds done or not done. When our identity is challenged, defending ourselves is a natural response. Pradeep, Ursula, and Ike, quite predictably, went on the defensive.

- "'Productive.' Are you kidding me? I'm the last one to leave this office most days."

- "'Ease up.' Yeah, right. No one else does anything around here. If I didn't do it, chaos would reign."

- "'She's partying and doesn't miss me a bit. I know she wanted more attention, but with her, it's never enough. I was doing the best I could. And the workload at the office is killing me."

As these examples show, the fight with the other points to the fight with the self. We fight from the outside in. Why did the word *productive* keep ringing in Pradeep's ears? If he had absolutely no question about how productive he is, it wouldn't have hung around all day in his head and gut. But his manager hit a live wire. Prior to this, Pradeep kept lists of what he had accomplished to prove his accomplishments to himself and to his manager. He's worried that he isn't productive enough.

Ursula makes a case for why she *can't* ease up: she lives with a house full of sloths. She isn't uptight, she's just doing what has to be done. Someone has to be responsible. But the comment stuck. She couldn't help but notice the wrinkles developing around her pursed lips.

Ike tells himself how much he loves his wife and though he's guilty of several mistakes, he doesn't believe they were as big as she made them out to be. But secretly he remembers how many hours he had whiled away watching porn late at night after his wife went to bed, even though she begged him to join her.

In each case, the person is thrown into internal conflict by the external conflict. They fight a core perception of who they are: the self they do not want to be. Pradeep does not want to be unproductive; Ursula doesn't want to be uptight; and Ike doesn't want to be an insufficient husband. Though each person is forced by the other to touch briefly that uncomfortable place within, each rebounds just as quickly, frantically defending themselves.

External conflict brings into focus that part of ourselves we don't want to see—what we've pushed away to keep a semblance of comfort with ourselves. The external conflict forces us to look at the internal struggle that we've neglected. The problem is that in neglecting our inner conflict, we don't make it go away, and suppressing it requires valuable energy. Pradeep defends his productivity; Ursula tries to convince herself she's not uptight; and Ike stubbornly maintains that he was a good enough partner. Each wastes energy in doing so.

Just as the fight with the other points to the fight with self, the corollary is also true: the fight with self requires us to fight with the other from the inside out. We're attracted to the fight within, and the conflict with the other helps us work through that inner fight. Here are some examples of how internal and external conflicts relate.

Our expectations sometimes create fights. We have an expectation that something should happen or that someone shouldn't do something. Our expectations may be realistic or unrealistic, fair or unfair, necessary or unnecessary, but they often create difficulty for us. We put pressures on others to conform to our expectations so that we don't have to deal with our fears. For example, I might put pressure on my child to act in a certain manner so that I look like a good mother and don't have to address that troubling question, "Am I a good parent?"

Or perhaps placing expectations on the other allows us to overcome a fear and, at the same time, pushes the other along in a necessary, healthy direction. For example, I fear being a nag like my mother, but I also have the expectation that I and my partner should share equally in household chores. In this case, confronting my partner about his spending too much time on the couch could be a dicey, possibly drawn out process—hopefully with a win-win result. He can shift his role and ultimately feel better about himself in the home, and I discover a way to get what I need without being a nag. Expectations are telling; they bring us back to self and create the opportunity to deal with our own restlessness. (For more about expectations, see Chapters 13, 14, and 15.)

We may need approval. We are often more dependent on the other for approval than we would like, but if we're pleasers, this works quite well—until we unconsciously choose a spouse who is critical or find ourselves in a job with a scolding boss. In these situations, regardless of what we do, the other is still bent on criticizing us. We are forced to find a way of giving to ourselves what we had hoped to get from the other. We can move from valuing most what the other thinks of us to focusing on what we think of ourselves (unless we go on the hunt to engage in a similar scenario elsewhere).

We may have a negative character trait, such as lack of self-discipline, lack of motivation, or laziness. When we've spent several days in front of the TV and haven't accomplished much, we cannot help getting down on ourselves. Even though we want to act, we can't quite seem to find the motivation. This is where our internal struggle is assisted by an external struggle. When the other takes issue with any of these behaviors, we are pressed to take some action that will lessen the conflict within and without. The real stuff of conflict usually has less to do with what's going on between us and the other and more to do with what the other has triggered in us.

The Significant Role of the Other

As wretched as it feels, the other takes us not where we want to go but where we *need* to go. We wouldn't get there without them (which is a rather sobering thought). Conflict with the other hits upon a part of our identity that causes us stress—because, as with Pradeep, Ursula, and Ike, it reveals something about who we are that we don't want to be, or who we are not but want to be.

Conflict with the other provides the impetus for us to do battle with ourselves so that we can embrace ourselves like never before. Our inner struggle was first created in relationship and eventually finds its healing in relationship as well. Thus, the person who is our undoing can help to free us from our inner struggle.

Fighting for Change

Since fighting often has a negative connotation, let's look at why we fight. Some fights are necessary and others aren't. Fighting with the other to avoid the greater pain of dealing with the parts of ourselves that hold us back is not a good reason for a fight. Focusing on the other's shortcomings distracts us from looking at our own insecurities. But the short-term relief of blaming the other eventually gives way to chronic restlessness. Repeatedly defending our sensitivity results in unnecessary conflict.

On the other hand, there are several good reasons for a fight. Sometimes a situation calls for it: there's too much to lose by not taking an oppositional stance. Many parents find that their fighting is at an all-time high when their children are teenagers. One parent takes issue with the other, fearing that words spoken and consequences imposed on their child will fracture one or both parents' relationship with the adolescent. The fight for them, though unwelcome, is still preferable to the perceived risks. We fight because it's too costly not to fight.

We also fight to protect our primary relationships. This may sound counterintuitive, but think about the consequences of *not* addressing an issue. Suppose there's an incident and you conclude that your partner is a liar and not to be trusted; that your colleague takes the credit that's your due; or that your sibling is just out for himself. If you don't have a fight with the other, you harbor negative judgments about them. However, if you address the issue with the other, you may discover that your conclusion is wrong because you lacked sufficient information. Or you might decide that your conclusion is right, but at least now, because you have addressed the issue, the other has the chance to work toward a change that creates hope for the future. Or, at minimum, you can make choices based on a more accurate view of reality. In contrast, not having the conversation about the enduring frustration—not facing up to potential conflict—limits intimacy in love relationships and inhibits effectiveness with those at work.

In addition, we're attracted to the fight with the other because we care about the future. Though it's informed by the past and we experience conflict in the present, a fight is really about what's to come. Bringing the tension of the future into the present produces the most powerful and enduring conflict. For example, I'm having this fight now because I fear that the other will cheat on me, break a promise, or humiliate me *again*. This troubling interaction is much too significant to forget and must be the impetus to change the pattern—which makes our struggle to grant forgiveness understandable.

Sometimes a fight becomes the marker that separates the past from the future. I remember once saying after an altercation, "What I know is that this can't happen again. I don't like who I am and I don't like what this does to me or to our relationship." And that was enough for the moment. Even if we're not certain what change we'll make behaviorally next time, determining that the pattern cannot continue begins to shape a different future.

Conflict always nudges us in the direction of change (even if the change is accepting what is). Our difficulty with conflict is really our challenge in knowing how to change ourselves. The forces that conspire to keep us in the same place are often sturdier and more gripping than the delicate, vulnerable shoots of change.

The Value of Conflict

Since there is a push in our society today to assess, understand, and resolve conflict, it looks like we as individuals and organizations are on the right, proactive track. And though rapid resolution of conflict might be a good option some of the time, it might also be a sophisticated way of avoiding the real conflict. I caution against resolving conflict too quickly. Instead, I recommend increasing your capacity for conflict because of its potential value. The true value of conflict is that we get to face ourselves while we engage with the other. If we can embrace the tension it causes within and between us, conflict becomes a window into self *and* relationship. It reveals truths that the rest of life is generally reluctant to reveal.

If you come to see the value of conflict (or even become intrigued by its potential), it will change how you engage it. During conflict, if you are curiously looking for its worth, you are already activating your rational brain, even while your primal brain reacts instinctively. Looking for conflict's value increases your odds of a good outcome, because in doing so you interrupt your automatic stress response, which usually creates more problems than it solves. (For more on this, see Chapter 3.)

So, What Now?

We are attracted to those conflicts that hold something valuable for us. Try the following:

- Reflect on your last significant fight. Become curious about what value there might be for you in that conflict.

- Use the *fight between* to become curious about the *fight within*. What sensitivity or self-doubt is attracting you to this conflict?

- Notice the hurtful word spoken by the other instead of dismissing it, and let it shed light on what important part of you feels threatened.

CHAPTER 2

The Dilemma of Avoidance

The train traveling from New York City to Long Island was about three-quarters full of mostly quiet people. Some were reading, some were daydreaming, and, thankfully, some were plugged into their smartphones. My three daughters and I were barely nestled in for the ride when, as they bantered, one of them said to another, "You're high maintenance." ("Oh no—right now—when we're in the confines of a train?" I thought.) Two of the girls plunged into a heated dialogue, while my third daughter opted for her usual coping mechanism—she had perfected the art of falling asleep within sixty seconds to avoid messy situations. I was flummoxed, not knowing what my parental role should be at this point: "Do I try to intervene? I have been woefully unsuccessful at that in the past, so what would be different this time? The girls are older now. Maybe it's time I assume a new role ..." I decided to witness rather than participate. The discomfort for all of us was palpable. We were in a scary place—going down a perilous track without knowing what the outcome would be.

Valid Reasons for Avoiding Conflict

The out-of-control feeling activated when our identity is being threatened feels like confirmation enough that conflict should be avoided. Often we don't even know what sets off the strong reaction within, so how can we possibly convey it to another, let alone in a manner they can understand? Language is our best tool to address conflict, but words can confuse as much as they make clear and conceal as much as they reveal. Often we can't find the right words, because during negatively heightened arousal, speech production is inhibited.

Our opponent presents a formidable challenge. If we didn't think that, it wouldn't be a significant conflict. Opponents come in many forms and sometimes they switch from one form to another. There's the adversary who frequently blows up, lashes out, and is forceful or abusive. The tricky, slippery player uses words to charm and disarm, and though he or she utters comforting and reassuring words, nothing changes. Sometimes, with a manipulative foe, we only realize after the fact that we've been had. There's the Teflon opponent who doesn't let anything stick. A stonewalling match gives us nothing and possibly renders us powerless. Any of these various traits might inhibit our engagement with the conflict.

We also avoid conflict because we know how bad it can get when addressing the conflict will ensure only more of it, with no guarantee of a rewarding outcome. Cast a multigenerational glance over your own past, or that of someone you know, and you'll see that sometimes contact between parties is broken forever. Sometimes the other punishes us by disengaging, becoming cool and aloof. The other has power to hold out on us: maybe we lose a share in the family cabin, inclusion in the will, or a promotion at work. Maybe the other gets back at us for speaking up by sulking, pouting, or becoming grumpy. Or perhaps they lash out in a piercing anger, uttering words that remain etched in our memory. Significant in our life, the other has the capacity to inflict deep and lasting wounds. Bad experiences with conflict only reinforce a paradigm that it isn't good for us.

Another major detractor from engaging the conflict is that we often don't understand what the real problem is. Though in the example at the beginning of this chapter, "high-maintenance" was invoked as a possible behavioral irritant in my family, the real problem, triggered for each of us separately, was much more difficult to name. Naming is difficult, partly because we operate unconsciously much of the time. Only a small part of the brain is devoted to conscious awareness. Yet the unconscious drives behaviors, thoughts, and feelings. Making connections between these three is challenging. Most of us believe ourselves to be more self-aware than we actually are.

Since the negative emotion aroused by conflict is so intense, we feel desperate to solve the problem as quickly as possible. Our discomfort pushes us back to the certainty of what we know about the problem—but therein lies the rub. For example, we might decide that the other is a difficult person who regularly violates boundaries. We look for a solution that fits with that outlook. We might choose to stay away from the boundary-buster and that action—or solution—is deceptively helpful because it offers temporary relief. Unfortunately, it is a Band-Aid solution that doesn't deal with the real problem.

Resolution of the conflict often lies in discovering and addressing a newly identified problem. Yet that real problem lies outside our current understanding of the situation. What really bothers us about the boundary violator? Often, it's our own inability to set internal boundaries when we're with that individual—and that has everything to do with our identity struggle. Getting at the real conflict requires a paradigm shift and a challenge to current constructs. That might entail questioning a long-held belief, turning logic upside down, or questioning a comforting rationale. It might mean making connections and seeing patterns between behaviors—ours and theirs—that then change the way we view our interactions with the other.

In most cases, getting at the real problem—the actual source of conflict—will feel counterintuitive. The tendency during nettlesome times is to move faster in the same direction rather than to change direction. Questioning both the formulation of the problem and the expected solution creates instability and unpredictability, which helps to explain why we shy away from doing so.

Legitimizing Avoidance with the Hurting Line

When I'm helping a client find a way through conflict, I might say to them, "Have you spoken to her about this, or have you had the conversation?" The phrase I frequently hear back is the classic "hurting line": "I don't want to hurt her." (Or him or them.)

We have such a strong aversion to conflict that our mind works overtime to convince us of what it believes to be a "capital T Truth," when really it might simply be the easiest truth to absorb. "I don't want to hurt you," is the belief we feed ourselves, giving it a privileged position in our own heads. Yet we might be using a hurting line to justify our avoidance of conflict and, as a result, miss the other truths.

What do any of the hurting lines really mean? At some level, it could be that we really don't want to hurt the other. But an unacknowledged and sometimes unconscious hurting line might also exist: "I don't want to hurt you," could really mean "I'm afraid of being hurt." Intuitively we know that if we speak up, words or actions from the other will be coming right back at us, and that's the part we're unwilling to deal with. Our reasoning might be that we don't want to risk spoiling the evening, or the weekend for that matter. In addition, we may use a hurting line while harming the other by nursing our own pain. Yet we fail to acknowledge this to ourselves.

Hurting lines point to the layering and complexity of our responses to potential conflict. Which one is it? "I don't want to hurt you," "I don't want to get hurt," or "I want to hurt you." Or is it all three? Often, we hurt the other more in the long term by *not* addressing the issue between us. It's not that we mean to deceive. It's just that we are so easily deceived by ourselves. So, engaging conflict successfully—the central premise of this book—requires us to turn our gaze inward and challenge our ingrained self-deceptions.

Desiree and Thomas: Avoidance is Costly

Desiree has been bothered for a long time that her husband, Thomas, has diverse interests that leave little time for her and their family. As a partner in a law firm, Thomas feels the ongoing pressures of cases and deadlines. His commitment to physical fitness is another priority that will not be compromised. Thomas also believes in giving back to the community and has been involved for years in a variety of church ministries. Desiree often feels like she's too far down on his list of priorities.

Occasionally when she is at Thomas's workplace or at church, Desiree hears people speaking highly of him. She can see that he feels appreciated and energized. In the recesses of her mind, when all this goes on around her, Desiree still feels sidelined and unimportant. Thomas seems to have time for everyone and everything else except her.

When Desiree listens to her own thoughts, they sound petty. She wants to be unselfish rather than selfish like her father. Surely, she should be happy that Thomas has found his niche and makes a valuable contribution. She wants to be a supportive wife and not begrudge him his success. When Thomas speaks eagerly about the next thing on his agenda, Desiree talks herself into taking the high road. She will not be a complainer. Yet despite her best efforts, unsettling thoughts still niggle away at her.

The struggle continues. Thomas comes home spent, needing rest and relaxation time. It seems easier for everyone when Desiree just slips into life on his terms. At times, she tries to assert her desires, but Desiree quickly loses her voice when Thomas makes a convincing pitch about how busy he is and how much stress he's under. There's also a disturbing voice in her head that says, "He doesn't even seem like the same person around here. He's moody and gets irritated easily."

In the past, Desiree has made some attempts at broaching the topic of feeling unimportant, but little progress occurs and, afterward, Thomas retreats for days. She contemplates raising her real feelings of discontent again, but is not sure that she's prepared to live with the consequences. Thomas has perfected the art of delivering disparaging comments with a warm smile, which makes Desiree crazy and confused. She also questions whether she has the right to ask for more, since Thomas's accomplishments have afforded her a rewarding lifestyle. Not only does she live in a spectacular home in a lovely part of town, but she also has the luxury of not working. How can she possibly demand time from him? And even though somewhere in her head she doesn't buy the "money equals power" equation, she feels distinctly disenfranchised because she's not bringing in cash. The imbalance in their financial contributions helps to constrict her vocal chords.

Desiree feels the tension inside her rising. When she is bursting with the need for an outlet, she talks to her sister, a friend, and her mother about Thomas's unavailability, and her comments are riddled with resentment and jealousy. The problem is that Desiree keeps most of her struggle away from Thomas, the very person she's at odds with. She decides to try to please a little more, be a little more upbeat, and maybe he will ache to be with her. Yet the more rope she gives, the more he seems to take.

What is the dilemma of avoidance for Desiree and Thomas?

- By avoiding the conflict, their relationship is more peaceful in the short term. There are no "drag on, drag it out" fights, at least not on the surface. Thomas thinks, "All is well." Superficial peace is seductive and deceiving. How fine are things, really?

- Desiree experiences tension regardless. She has the double challenge of feeling all is not well *and* working out the problem on her own. She has exchanged a modicum of peace on the outside for increased internal conflict. Though the marital front is somewhat peaceful, Desiree is becoming increasingly impatient with their children, because when conflict is not addressed at its source, it begs for an outlet elsewhere.

- Desiree makes numerous attempts to remove her discomfort and pain by increasing her commitments elsewhere. She enrols in a yoga class and joins a reading club. But her coping strategies don't address the real problem.

- Avoiding conflict often brings a physical response, which is difficult to ignore. Desiree's doctor prescribes her an anti-anxiety medication. (The body speaks for us when we cannot.)

- Avoiding the struggle does not result in a holding pattern. Rather, avoidance leads to a situation of diminishing returns. Desiree begins to distance herself from Thomas, and he feels this.

- Desiree's sister, mother, and friend become collateral damage. They are caught up in the hurtful situation. As people who care for her and want her happiness, they listen intently to her troubles and rack their brains to come up with helpful suggestions, yet they are powerless to affect change.

- Thomas is a formidable opponent, which is enough to discourage Desiree from addressing the issues between them. In his early days, he excelled on the debate team and he has never been known to give up easily. Shifting their relationship will be difficult. Yet at the same time, Thomas really wants to have a good marriage and he is not comfortable with being self-absorbed. Desiree will have to courageously take a stand and hold her own.

- Both Desiree and Thomas continue to be pushed around by their own insecurities, because neither is forced to confront them. Desiree feels "less than" and unimportant. By not standing up sufficiently for herself, she's destined to maintain that struggle. Thomas has not been forced to face the constant need for approval that causes him to endlessly strive. Over time he only becomes more selfish because his selfishness is inadvertently being fed by the relationship patterning the two of them have implicitly agreed upon.

Individually and as a couple, Desiree and Thomas are living with more pain than is necessary. Then Desiree meets someone who wakes her up, wrests her from the stalemate, and she is forced to make a difficult decision about whether to overhaul her marriage or end it.

Perhaps as you were reading this case study you thought that Desiree should simply stand up for herself. But Desiree is not only fighting herself and her dearly held value of not being selfish like her father, she is also fighting her cultural and communal contexts, which say that she should not be a demanding wife. In addition, she knows that asserting herself would increase conflict between her and Thomas because he would resist the change.

Our reticence to engage in conflict is only overcome by the cost of not doing so. For Desiree, the combination of her mental health crisis and the potential of devoted love elsewhere propels her to challenge the status quo in her marriage. She can no longer afford to block out her soul's rumbling. While she avoids conflict with Thomas, Desiree evades a deeper conflict within herself.

We can usually make a strong case for avoiding conflict. Yet here is the dilemma: if we avoid the conflict, we remain stuck. Significant conflict does not simply disappear, and circumventing it costs us in at least three ways. First, even if we don't have the fight with the other, we're still having it in our own heads. Without even meaning to, we're building a case against the other. So avoiding the external conflict does not bring us peace. Second, avoiding conflict requires a considerable investment of time and energy. For example, think about attending a party, work function, or family gathering where you have an ongoing conflict with another attendee. Throughout the event you will likely be aware of where that person is, who they are talking to, and how others are responding to them. You may be manoeuvring to stay outside their physical orbit. That's a lot of work and detracts from your experience of the event. The creative energy expended on avoiding the conflict often outweighs the emotional energy required to face the person and work it through. Third, because the conflict has not been eradicated, it is free to re-emerge at will, leaving us vulnerable still.

As with Desiree and Thomas, the collateral damage of avoided conflict is underappreciated. The fallout affects not just you and the person you're in conflict with. The people who care about you feel your tension intently and it becomes their tension too. Think about how many mothers or fathers stand between the other parent and their children. Consider how many siblings stand between other warring siblings, or employees between colleagues in workplaces where tension is mounting.

When Conflict Comes to Us

Sometimes we find ourselves in a situation in which we're compelled to act. Not to do so would be against our own value system, which ultimately makes us feel like there's no choice but to act. We are in such a situation when tensions escalate between our spouse and child. We are in it when we hear what we know is a lie, or see the wrong person take the credit. The situation itself cries for a voice. Otherwise, in a strange way, we are complicit. We don't relish acting on this circumstance because we know all too well that speaking up comes with a cost. However, conflict calls forth a somewhat scary, yet possibly the best, part of our humanity. Will we or will we not weigh in? Either we expose the injustice for what it is and it stops with us, or we perpetuate it. To be soulfully human is to get dirty.

The hard reality is that we will get tarnished in the process of conflict. Even if initially we feel as if we're fighting someone else's battle, somewhere along the line it becomes ours too. Entering the fray, we might intensify and complicate the battle further. Since conflict is never clean and is mostly messier than we hope it will be, we'll often be tempted to forgo the opportunity it affords.

Missed Opportunity

You might be so averse to conflict that in your continual stepping away, you don't even know you're in it. Or you shut down possible conflict by becoming a master at adaptation and accommodation. Perhaps you settle for a lacklustre marriage or uninspiring family relationships because you fear having potentially risky conversations. You have given up your opportunity to go after a vigorous, life-giving relationship and have settled instead for mediocrity because it affords a measure of safety. But if you give up, or never engage, then it's over: avoiding conflict is completely understandable, but significant conflicts don't disappear. They resurface at will, so avoiding them only perpetuates more.

So, What Now?

We avoid conflict because of the fear, discomfort, and pain of engaging with it; yet by avoiding the conflict, the pain remains. Try the following:

- Still thinking of your own significant fight, acknowledge to yourself your desire to run when the tension between you increases.

- Push the pause button and view what is happening within you from a bird's eye perspective, one step removed.

- Stay with the out-of-control feeling that comes up until you understand it more, because that's your best chance of also gaining control of yourself.

- If you can, stay engaged a little longer than you would have previously.

CHAPTER 3

Why Don't We Learn
from our Conflict?

Since learning from conflict necessitates at least short-term pain, we become quite resourceful at adopting methods to avoid the pain of facing ourselves. But unfortunately, these methods are problematic because not only do they fail to remove the inner turmoil, they also feed the fight with the other. Though we may have built-in brain-traps that inhibit learning from conflict, we can retrain our minds and use them as a tool to do conflict better.

Which Methods Do You Use?
This section details the various strategies we employ to avoid facing our inner turmoil—from denial to justification to escapism—that allow us to dodge the pain rather than deal with its cause. Try to recognize which strategies you or people close to you use.

Convincing the other. Perhaps the other accuses you of needing to be right, being self-absorbed, or being two-faced. In response, you might over-explain yourself, argue that your actions are understandable considering the extenuating circumstances, or try to convince the other that their perceptions are wrong—all the while hoping that the other will retract their hurtful words. If you can convince the other that they are wrong about you, then you don't have to face who you are.

Cutting the person out. In conflict, you might be inclined to cut the problematic person out of your life. Having limited or no contact is more difficult in some circumstances than in others and often comes with a cost. Suppose the problematic person is a family member. If it's your spouse, leaving the relationship is possible but will have ramifications that you must be prepared to live with, particularly when children are involved. But suppose the other is a colleague or, worse yet, your boss, and your success depends on a viable relationship. Suppose that leaving your place of work is not feasible. Now you are stuck.

Blaming self. Another possible strategy is to blame yourself. "I shouldn't have said this or done that. I just keep screwing up." Blaming yourself and blaming the other are quite similar, though they feel different. At first glance you might think that blaming yourself is the same as accepting personal responsibility, but this isn't necessarily so. Sometimes your quick and simple admission of culpability is just enough to make you feel better: "I know I lose my temper and say a lot of stupid things," you might say to yourself, but that acknowledgement doesn't lead to behavior changes. In addition, since blaming self is often accompanied by excessive guilt, reducing the guilt can become the focus rather than pursuing a constructive course of action to remedy the situation.

Escaping to distraction. Or perhaps, instead of cutting the person out or blaming yourself, you distract from the pain of facing yourself: "I feel like crap so I'll turn up the music in hope that I can drown out the voice in my head." You might get lost, for example, in a TV show, a compelling book, a great bottle of wine, or intense exercise. Sometimes a diversion is exactly what you need, for a time. However, if running away from yourself becomes a habitual pattern, nothing changes and the problem continues.

Denying the reality. Besides distraction, denial is another common escape from the pain of your inner conflict. You will not tolerate something that unsettles you, and instead you believe whatever you need to believe—whatever makes you feel better—whether this aligns with reality or not. You wipe out your fear and cope by blocking self-awareness. If you've given yourself over to a delusional system, you might not even see that you are living in denial.

While you transition to the next step, denial can occasionally help. Sometimes it serves as a temporary antidote to debilitating levels of anxiety or overwhelming unhappiness, until you build up sufficient strength to absorb the harsh reality of a troubling situation. Denial can be a coping strategy, to be used wisely and selectively in the short run only.

The problem with denial is that it causes more problems than it solves. Much of the pain of conflict can be avoided if we face the truth of self. Perhaps you really were fired because of incompetence rather than an impossible, miserable boss who could not be pleased. (Or maybe both reasons are true but you can only acknowledge the one.) Denying your role in miserable circumstances makes you vulnerable to similar situations in the future. Plus, denial easily morphs into self-deception, increasing the risk that the other person will no longer trust you, because they see what is going on even if you don't.

Justifying the situation. Sometimes justification is exactly what is necessary. A situation requires that we declare the good reasons for our actions. Other times we might be rationalizing or making excuses, even to ourselves, to improve the optics of an otherwise bad action. Sometimes we self-justify to quiet the cognitive dissonance within. With two opposing forces colliding in our brains, we eliminate one and focus on the other to attain inner peace.

Recall the last time you were triggered by someone and reflect on how hard you worked to justify yourself. "Let me tell you why," perhaps you said. Or, "If I tell you this, then you'll get it." The justification schemes can be quite elaborate. You might buttress your position with a belief system that is difficult to challenge. With your God (or tradition or the government) on your side, you stand courageously. The black-and-white world conveniently obliterates the gray. Alternatively, you might use the other's actions to justify your own: "My partner isn't into sex and I've got to get it somewhere," you tell yourself, legitimizing cheating instead of pressing deeper into the underlying issues that separate the two of you. Or you think, "My employer isn't paying me enough, so I can bill for unworked hours."

Self-justification shields us from seeing what we don't want to see about ourselves. Like denial, it is such an automatic response that we might not even know we're doing it until someone else challenges us about it. The cost of justification is that it allows us to turn away from our part in something that failed (an interaction or a broken relationship, for example) thus diluting the potential of learning from our mistakes—something that might be helpful for us in the long term. What breakthroughs would be possible if we refused to justify shortcomings?

Taking the high road to nowhere. There is yet another avoidance strategy you may use in conflict: taking the offensive behavior of the other in stride, managing to stay positive, and responding in a manner that appears surprisingly mature. To others, you look good. The other lashes out with some spiteful remarks, and you respond calmly, empathetically, about the source of their anger. But though your reaction might look appropriate and carry with it some moral advantages, you are using this strategy to avoid facing a "not so pretty" truth. You ignore the gritty interchange, sugarcoat the issues, and focus on an idealized future. The other feels that your response is not authentic and doesn't trust it. You take the imagined high road, which leads you nowhere, because you are afraid to go where the real road will take you.

Committing to good management. This strategy is to develop good management skills, navigate the testy interactions well, and stay out of trouble. By reading books or attending training workshops you anticipate the pitfalls of conflict and avoid them. You are committed to learning the skills of having a difficult conversation—by either shutting your mouth or speaking up, whatever your challenge is. You are even willing to white-knuckle your way through, putting on your best behavior. You focus on preventing conflict and limiting the damage. These tactics sound good, except once again they bypass the real problem.

You appear to be "managing" conflict well, but nothing has changed for you on the inside. You are not addressing the part of yourself that causes the problem. Suppose your partner has an issue with your ongoing demeaning or negative commentary. In the interest of harmony, you decide to be civil and keep your comments to yourself, but you refuse to examine your offensive internal commentary and where it's coming from. And since being on good behavior is not sustainable, that critical part of you cannot help but stir up trouble again. Good management hides the dirt and prevents you from dealing with it. Simply managing conflict at the surface level isn't enough.

Likely we have used all the strategies described above at one time or another. They are seductive because they help us cope, to a certain degree. They temporarily take the edge off the pain but it ultimately remains.

Most of Us Are Too Good at Coping
One of the reasons that our pain and conflict endures for years is because we are good at coping with our problems—rather too good. Our coping behavior makes sense to us. Sometimes the problem just seems insurmountable. Other times we have become anaesthetized to the costs of the unresolved conflict and recognize them only when too much time has passed (and, for example, a partner is ready to move out). Or perhaps we have surrendered to a defeatist belief such as "Life (or marriage) is just like this and pain is unavoidable."

We get so good at coping with our problems that we no longer feel any urgency to deal with them. But eventually our coping methods create new problems. Focusing *beside* the problem rather than acting *on* the problem makes us vulnerable: we will continue to be threatened by the same issues. Rather than harnessing conflict for personal change, the status quo becomes entrenched.

Let's now look at why it can be challenging to use conflict to learn about ourselves and the other.

When We Feel Threatened, Learning from Conflict Is Difficult
In describing a conflict, a client will often say, "It was such a stupid little thing." Though it may appear like a stupid little thing, if it unsettles your innards, then it is likely connected to something that really matters and, therefore, is not a stupid little thing at all. We get worked up when we feel threatened at some level. Almost instantly, a fight moves from being outside, between us and the other, to being inside our being. When a fight moves inside, it becomes much more difficult to tolerate.

When we're feeling threatened, the automatic response is to attempt to take the fight back outside—to prove to the other (and to ourselves) that we're not the problem. We might create a story about the other, such as, "With his controlling and abrasive nature, everyone has problems with him." Doing so takes the edge off our feeling of being out of control, temporarily absolves us of blame, and soothes our rankled nerves. Self-righteousness sneaks in. The story makes sense to us, in part, because we're blind to our own contribution to the conflict (or invested in not seeing it). Building a one-sided story comes easily when we're feeling threatened.

Threats can be confusing. Though we feel a need to protect ourselves, how to do so is not always clear. Should we walk toward or away from the fight? Both are a means to the same end—to avoid a threat to self. Yet either action may have the same outcome: approaching or avoiding the threat of the other might increase the threat to self.

Add one more layer of confusion: conflict is not always as it appears. What seems life sustaining at the outset often turns upside down midstream and ultimately becomes threatening. But the opposite can also be true. Partners may opt for what appears life sustaining and forgo the difficult conversations, yet the outcome is the breakup of the partnership (threat realized). Or the converse can happen: partners engage in threatening conversations and the outcome is a more vital, stronger relationship.

Take another example. Suppose the other repeatedly mistreats you. In the immediate, challenging that behavior can feel threatening, especially if you think the other will resist you. Yet not to confront the behavior means that, over time, you're at risk of thinking less of yourself. Approach and avoidance are always options when dealing with threat, and they both hold risk. Being hardwired to avoid conflict *and* to engage it at the same time can feel like faulty wiring—which causes even more conflict and confusion. Now let's explore in detail how the wiring of our brains can serve to confuse us.

Brain conflict. Perhaps we have been entrapped by our own evolution—or lack of it. Our reactions to conflict have a base in physiology. The amygdala (which one client affectionately refers to as "Ole Iggy"), in the limbic system, is designed to protect us during perceived threats. Vigilance for danger, reacting to threats, and quick responses are adaptive behaviors that historically increased our chances for survival. (In the jungle, the days of a laid-back animal are numbered.) The amygdala is impressive, answering a perceived threat in approximately one hundred milliseconds; whereas the rational brain, the neocortex, takes anywhere from five hundred to six hundred milliseconds to process the experience. (For more information on this topic, see Louis Cozolino's *The Neuroscience of Psychotherapy.*) Yet, left to its own devices, the ever-vigilant amygdala creates quite the mess. Lashing out or retreating in fear rarely produces satisfactory outcomes.

There is another problem. Although Ole Iggy doesn't necessarily function well on its own, it doesn't play well with others either. The primitive brain could work with the more evolved rational brain, but instead each one fights for dominance. We could say that the tensions are written right into their job descriptions: the amygdala's role is to warn us of danger and the rational brain's job is to assess whether Ole Iggy is right. Is the fear warranted? The fight between the areas in the brain feels unfair, because the primitive brain is agile and compelling whereas the more civilized rational brain is sluggish and doubtful in comparison. Yet frequently the primitive brain gets into trouble and needs to be reined in by the rational brain. Keeping a healthy balance between the two is no small feat.

But the brains can develop a healthy interdependence, informing and shaping each other, navigating the conflict. The limbic system, through its quick and strong reactions, invites the neocortex to increase consciousness and expand self-awareness, discovering what insecurities drive the triggers; the amygdala highlights what the neocortex would like to ignore. If we don't use the neocortex to revisit the painful place within that begs for attention, then we may slip into rationalization and self-delusion. In a complementary relationship, the neocortex works with the limbic system to challenge the learnings and memories of the past, thereby creating new neural connections. As the neocortex learns to reinterpret the limbic information, new options become available. Although the two have different roles, they collaborate, cooperate, and work toward integration with each other, such that their roles truly become complementary. This integration does not come naturally; it requires us to apply the mind as we listen to and seriously consider the input of each brain. This is the reflective work of navigating conflict—the essence of this book.

It is also possible that the two brains work together to *not* deal with conflict. Ole Iggy picks up any perceived threat to self-identity and tries to shut it down. If the sensitivities activated are also too much for the rational brain to handle, then it copes cognitively by simply removing the threat (the other person or situation, for instance) rather than working through it. The unfortunate consequence is that the vulnerability remains and nothing changes. Sadly, this is a common experience for many. When the neocortex serves us well, it increases self-awareness by realistically assessing the threat and, ultimately, devising a plan to deal with it.

Here is the hope: even though we function with a built-in brain-trap that keeps us stuck in conflict, we can learn to use the mind as a powerful tool to deal with, or even delay, the trigger. Even when the amygdala quickly dominates, we don't have to be held hostage by the limbic system.

The concepts in this book will help you turn the trap into a tool. You will come to understand why you get triggered and, once you know, the frequency or intensity of being triggered, decreases. This book helps you recognize your red flags—the thoughts that shift you from the neocortex to the limbic system. When your limbic system takes over, that is an early warning sign that your restless, wounded identity has been triggered. Your thoughts are highly unique and personal, though they likely challenge you in the general areas of security and/or significance. Changing how you think about conflict strengthens the neocortex function and helps you manage your limbic system. The two brains can work in concert to promote the healing of your sensitivities.

Recognizing that the mind can be used as a tool creates not just a little shift, but rather results in a quantum leap in our capacity for engaging conflict effectively. We begin to experience neuroplasticity at work and have hope for the journey ahead.

This book provides a critical path and helps us coach our neocortex to harness the primitive brain while in conflict with others, and as we do so, we also learn more about our inner conflict.

Trusting the Conflict Process

Though conflict takes you down an unpredictable road, "trusting the process" during conflict is the best mindset. It keeps us open to and intrigued by what is taking place. We willingly surrender to the journey because we believe that it will reveal what we need to see and take us where we need to go. Trusting the process comes with the following six benefits.

Nurtures life-giving beliefs. Beliefs either hold us back or free us up. When we believe conflict has value, we experience it differently, which is why the first part of this book is devoted to challenging our thinking about conflict. If we trust that staying with the pain instead of running from it is the best way to work through it and leave it behind, we endure, because we see an end. If we believe that this trying experience is an essential step in producing change for the future, it becomes a necessary hardship. If we know that we are going to be okay no matter what happens, we look forward in faith rather than being bound up in fruitless fear.

Prepares us for an adventure. Valuable finds are bound up in a riddle. When we're lost, we get just enough clues to reassure us that we are indeed on track. Our heightened reaction informs us that we are close to something significant. When we get worked up and feel the pain, we know that staying with it rather than quickly moving on will yield benefits. Though viewing the other as the problem is tempting, we know that turning the gaze on ourselves changes our lives.

Contains or minimizes fear. Trusting the process is one way of capping conflict's fuel: fear, which, if not addressed, takes over. Fear is like the monster that lives under the bed until the child dares to confront it: in bending down to look directly into the eyes of the monster, the child makes it shrivel up and disappear. In a similar way, trusting the conflict process enables us to look right at fear and cut it down to size.

Softens unhelpful resistance in us. A fighting attitude is sometimes exactly what is needed to overcome life's challenges. If we have the resolve or the grit to resist the disagreeable antics of the other, we have the capacity to break unhelpful conflict patterns. If, on the other hand, we resist the painful experiences that could result in personal transformation, then that resistance ultimately hurts us. Trusting the process helps us surrender to the uncomfortable instead of wasting our energy resisting that which keeps us in the same frustrating place.

Fosters curiosity. Probably the single greatest benefit of trusting the conflict process is that it infuses us with an expectant sense of curiosity. We take note with keen interest, observe what is going on in us, speculate about what might be going on for the other, and respect that the situation we are in emerges in a context that is bigger than either of us. We question: "What will happen this time?" Rather than attaching ourselves to a plan, we settle on one or two helpful directional statements, such as, "When I feel the negative charge, I'll take a bathroom break to figure out *what I feel about me*, and then do something/anything about it." Or "This time I won't run like before."

Challenges and builds hope. The conflict process can challenge hope, because sometimes when we believe that this time will be different, we get more of the same. Hope is dashed with "It's the same old stuff and nothing's changed." Maybe you disappoint yourself by falling into similar traps or patterns. Maybe you are disappointed because, when you are primed to act differently, no opportunity presents itself. Curiosity, the companion of hope, gets snuffed out by lack of opportunity. Perhaps when you had hoped for an opening in the sky, it looks lifelessly drab.

Yet hope trumps hopelessness because if there is time and life, there is the possibility of a better outcome. The sky is forever changing. If we believe in the process, we know that something will be birthed from this too, even when we cannot yet see it.

Once you begin gleaning valuable takeaways from the fight, you will become a believer in the process. As much as you can, focus on being in control of you—not of what is happening inside you—but by behaving in a way that is consistent with whom you want to be. Having addressed your thinking about conflict, you are prepared to *use* the conflict with the other to work through your inner conflict.

So, What Now?

To learn from your conflict, face pain instead of simply coping with it, examine the threat rather than fleeing from it, use the mind as a powerful tool to deal with the trigger, and trust the conflict process, because it takes you where you need to go. Try the following:

- Identify one coping method you are using right now to avoid facing something uncomfortable about yourself. If you can't identify one, ask your friends for help, because they likely witness your patterns.

- When you feel yourself getting worked up in a conflict, ask yourself what part of your identity feels threatened. Understanding your reactivity is key to coaching your primitive brain during conflict.

- Despite its discomfort, see if you can surrender to the conflict journey—just be in the mess—and become curious about where it might take you.

PART 2
USING THE FIGHT
WITH THE OTHER

*Fights trigger the deeper conflicts you have within yourself.
Since fighting with the other is easier than facing the unwanted
parts of yourself, you inadvertently keep the fight going and
your inner turmoil continues.*

CHAPTER 4

Five Familiar Conflict Tunes

Can you name your conflict tune? Or perhaps your relationship is accompanied by several recurring refrains. This chapter explores several common themes that can trigger conflict, from "You're Being Defensive" to "Don't Take It Personally" to the dreaded "Power Struggle." We'll look at why these conflicts tend to go round and round, and at how you can begin to lower the volume on your own "favorite songs."

You're Being Defensive

How often have you heard someone say, "You're being defensive"? Or how often have you thought someone *else* was being defensive? (Note: Defensiveness is always easier to recognize in another person.) Sometimes the defensiveness is blatant and in-your-face. Other times it is subtler. Here are some examples of defensive statements and their possible purpose:

- "I can never please you." (This could protect the speaker from looking at legitimate issues.)

- "No matter what I do, it won't make a difference." (This comment might really mean, "I don't have to do a thing!")

- "You always do it your own way, anyway." (This could be an underhanded technique designed to discredit the other.)

While the word defensiveness typically carries a negative connotation, being defensive sometimes serves a legitimate purpose. We become defensive to help us manage anxiety, cover up the hurt we've absorbed, and fend off any more that may be coming our way. We're not talking here about minor hurts, but rather injuries to the essence of who we think we are, which create a threat to our very identity. Here are two healthy uses of defensiveness:

- *It can offer temporary protection from a cruel and hostile world.* The insensitive and sometimes cruel ways others treat us—both in early family life and through our adulthoods—can corrode the human psyche, leaving scars. Whether wittingly or unwittingly, we hurt our children, children hurt each other, and as adults, we see more fully the extent of our inability to protect them sufficiently. When others don't protect us, human beings find ways to protect themselves. We might put up walls, ready to fight even when there isn't an enemy on the other side. Yet the capacity for self-defense is a critical and normal part of development.

- *It can signal that something important is happening internally.* Defensiveness is worth paying attention to. The pushed-away, painful parts of ourselves (and others) usually emerge not in a nicely packaged form, but rather in the guise of off-putting defensiveness. When we pay attention, defensiveness can lead us directly to the fragile parts of both ourselves and the other.

Yet as helpful as it can be at times, defensiveness—especially when automatic and protracted—can be harmful. By and large, it deserves the bad rap it gets. Here are three negative aspects of defensiveness:

- It can keep your sensitivity hidden and then blindside you during conflict, which it in turn maintains.

- When inappropriate, it can start an unnecessary fight.

- It can be counterproductive when the environment in which it was necessary no longer exists and when it undermines health.

It's important to keep in mind, however, that standing up for yourself is important. During a difficult conversation, you need the other to hear your perspective or to correct their misinformation. Telling yourself that you want to "take the high road" by keeping quiet does nothing to help resolve conflict. Before speaking up, check your motivation with a question: "Am I illegitimately building a case to exonerate myself?" If you are not trying to absolve yourself of responsibility, seize the moment to rightfully speak your truth in a tone that promotes healing—rather than triggering the other person's defensiveness.

Don't Take It Personally

During conflict, the wisdom of taking it personally, or not, resides in discerning between *making it about you* and *it being about you*. As you explore the two positions, recall a couple of recent exchanges with another to identify your default tendency. (If you're not sure, ask a trusted friend.) Then, reflect on how "taking it personally"—or not—might impact the other.

Making It About You

When the air goes heavy and thick around you, discovering if you're part of the problem could be critical to solving it. In such a scenario, *making it about you* potentially produces useful results. However, if you are feeling insecure and in regular need of attention or reassurance, you run the risk of making *everything* about you—you take it personally when it's unwarranted. (Your antennae chronically over-function. This is the opposite of the habitual reaction of the person in denial, who takes too little personally.) The danger here is in becoming so reactive that you cannot hear what's going on for the other person. When you take it personally, even if the other initiated the conversation, the focus shifts from them to you. Then neither of you benefits. You feel under attack and they feel that the real issue has gotten lost—and that they aren't being heard.

Making it about you is also a backward form of self-defense. You'd think that when you make it all about you, you'd be facing yourself more honestly, but the strategy doesn't seem to work out like that. Instead, you shift from focusing on the issue at hand to ridding yourself of injured feelings. You look for reassurance that you are okay, or at least "not that bad." You lose sight of the fact that the other is made to feel bad in the process—for inadvertently offending *you* with *their* issue. They end up with a double hurt, because they also don't feel heard. *Making it about you* is a way of controlling the conversation and closing it down on your terms.

It Is About You

Of course, sometimes the other person's upset *is* about you. When you pick up signals of disturbance from the other, you can find out whether you play a role in it with a simple question: "Did I do or say something to upset you?" If the answer is affirmative, the two of you can get to work on clearing the conflict.

"Is it about me?" is a courageous question because it willingly invites feedback that is not easy to hear. The other might come back with the particulars of "When you said…" or "When you did…" You discover your impact on the other and see that they view an incident differently than you do. Later in this chapter, we'll discuss what you might do with the feedback you receive.

Of course, the other may well respond to your opening question, "Is something wrong?" with the infamous "No. Nothing." (Yeah, right.) Occasionally that might be accurate, but more likely they're either not yet aware of what is bothering them or they are aware but unwilling to discuss it. They might be waiting for a little more coaxing from you. In such a case, you might follow up with something like, "Okay, but it feels to me like something *is* upsetting you. If and when you want to talk, I'm ready."

Sorting through the difference between *making it about you* and *it is about you* helps clarify if you're creating or solving problems. And if you're not sure of the distinction, ask the other (or a trusted friend) if you take it personally when it's not warranted, or if you miss it when really you are the problem.

It Wasn't My Intention

In working through a hurtful situation, how often have you heard (or said to the other): "That's not what I intended," or "I didn't mean it that way"? Sometimes you must work backward, trying to undo the impact of your words or actions on the other. At other times, the other person wants to assure you that the hurt incurred from their words or actions was not what they intended at all.

If it's a simple case of the message sent being different from the message received, one of two clarifying questions may suffice. If your words have caused hurt, you might say, "Did you hear me right?" If you felt injured by the other's words, you could ask, "Did I hear you right?" With these questions, you create a space for correction and a new understanding.

However, situations are usually a little more nuanced than that, because communication—and human beings—are multilayered. The space between intent and impact is worth exploring. Our view of a given situation can be cockeyed, because more often than not our intention is to see things in our own favor—even if we won't (or can't) admit this to ourselves. For example, we might say, "I was just trying to help you," and yet the other picks up on our critical and condescending tone.

Imposing a Double Standard

Desiring to look like the "good one" in interactions, we unknowingly hold double standards. In short, we are kinder to ourselves than we are to the other. As we become more aware of double standards, perhaps we will first laugh at ourselves and then change the way we view both ourselves and the other. Here are some typical double standards:

- In conflict, we judge the other by their impact on us. ("He hurt my feelings.") But we judge ourselves by our intentions. ("I'm trying to do good.")

- We attribute the other's hurtful impact on us to internal, personal factors. ("He is hot-tempered"; "she is inconsiderate.") By contrast, we tend to attribute our hurtful impact on the other to external factors. ("The stress at work has been enormous.")

- In the face of conflict, we tend to attribute the other's successes to external factors. ("Her dad's words forced her to face the undesirable consequences and make the right choice.") In contrast, when we feel successful at working through the conflict, we attribute it to who we are. ("It's because I'm a forgiving person.")

- The reverse is true when it comes to attributing reasons for failure. We attribute the other's failure to internal factors and our own shortcomings to external elements over which we have no control. If the other leaves a job due to conflict, we might say, "He doesn't have the stamina to hang in when the times are tough." When we quit a job, we might say, "I had to leave because my boss was impossible."

Double Standards Table

Standard	Other	Self
Judging intent and impact	By impact	By intent
Attributing hurtful impact	To internal factors	To external factors
Attributing success	To external factors	To internal factors
Attributing failure	To internal factors	To external factors

The trickiness of double standards points to the need to look deeper at the subtleties of intention. If you miss the undertone of your intention, you risk consequences both to yourself and the relationship. A few to consider:

- *You miss seeing a fuller you.* If you don't slow down and notice the undertones of your intention, you reduce yourself to one dimension and lose some of the depth and color that are part of a more complex identity. You will understand yourself in a much more limited way.

- *The other picks up your unintended truth.* The other person may be more intuitive than you imagine. When you say to them, "That's not what I intended," it may be true at one level. But could the other be picking up another, "small t" truth that you did not intend to communicate, because you wanted to conceal your real thoughts? You may not be aware of doing this; after all, you don't want to see yourself as a hurtful person. But the consequence may be a long-term injury to the relationship, because you can't mend what you can't, or don't want to, see.

- *Unacknowledged intentions keep the relationship stuck.* Actions and words are not always about good intentions, even when they appear as such on the surface. I can remember times in my marriage when I wanted to put my husband on edge because of the pain he had caused me. After a disagreement, I would innocently go shopping—but I wouldn't tell him when I was coming home, nor did I volunteer information about where I had been. It took me a while to recognize and name the passive-aggressive behavior for what it was. By acknowledging my less-than-honorable intentions, I created space for change within me and our relationship.

When You Hurt Each Other—What Next?

Let's look at three possible responses when the impact of words or deeds is hurtful. Either you or the other might be the offending party. You might:

- *Give the benefit of the doubt.* In a distressed relationship, each of you is filtering words and actions through past hurts. Therefore, be aware that your impact on the other will likely be negative, even if your intention was positive. (By contrast, in a more contented relationship characterized by trust, a positive intention is assumed.) Granting the benefit of the doubt is a powerful way to shift a troubled relationship in the direction of hope.

- *Identify the other's hostile intentions.* At the same time, not to recognize the other's hostile intention for what it is puts you at risk, because you fail to protect yourself. Hostile intentions need to be exposed for what they are. Ask the other, "Do you want to hurt me?" (Even though the other might answer with a hasty "no," your penetrating question is not easily dismissed.) If you have been hurt repeatedly by this person, it makes sense for you to think that the action was deliberate. Alternatively, the hurt might simply be the outcome of the other's self-protective behavior, or your misinterpretation of the interaction. Since intention will always be invisible, you must observe a person's actions over time and let behavioral patterns reveal the true feelings of the heart.

- *Take responsibility for the impact of your own words and actions.* Perhaps when you examine a comment perceived by the other as hurtful, you still think your intentions were good. But in the end, even the most genuine good intentions do not neutralize the impact.

If your impact on the other was negative, the interaction still needs be addressed and the other person's hurt feelings acknowledged.

Getting Feedback

When you invite feedback, you might yet bolster yourself with a little pep talk like, "I know I need feedback to get better at what I do." Getting *uninvited* feedback is another matter altogether. A common response to unsolicited feedback is to feel accused. The words might be direct, like "You're too controlling," or "You're overly sensitive," or the feedback might be more indirect, the other excluding or overlooking you. The feedback leaves you feeling like you are not enough of one thing and too much of something else.

We have an uncertain relationship with feedback. Do we trust it or do we not? We might think: Why is the other saying this? To what extent should I let it impact my view of who I am? The diagram below illustrates our almost automatic processing when we are trying to absorb feedback.

RESPONDING TO FEEDBACK

Feedback

Current view of self	Denial
Integration	Confusion

Adapted from Claes Janssen's *Four Room Apartment Model of Change*

Exit
(Back door)

39

At the upper left-hand corner of the diagram, we cling to a view of self that maintains our internal stability. But then new information enters in the form of feedback, represented by the arrow at the top of the diagram. We are told, "You are a soggy blanket," and we move to denial, in the upper right-hand quadrant, as almost a knee-jerk response ("I am not soggy and I am not a blanket. That's not how I view myself and it's not how others see me!") But if we stew on this feedback without dismissing it, it leads us to the bottom right-hand quadrant, where we're confused: "Soggy? What?" This is where we have a choice. We can discredit the speaker, dismiss the feedback, retreat through the exit door at the bottom of the confusion quadrant, and return to our original view of self, resuming the status quo and changing nothing.

Alternatively, we can stay with the confusion for a time and sort through what has merit and what does not. How is it that the other views us this way? What are we not seeing? Though we might rather be lighthearted, someone has confronted us with our oppressive air. How moody are we? In the lower left-hand quadrant, we integrate the feedback that fits; our view of self has been challenged and we recognize that we need to work on making a difficult change. All this gets integrated into a new view of who we are and who we want to become. A new norm settles in, until more feedback rattles us again. This is the ongoing process of personal change.

Power Struggle

Every relationship involves some aspect of power. From my perspective, thinking of power as a function of relationship maintains an awareness of power exchanges and imbalances, with the purpose of ensuring that each person feels adequately empowered. Reflect on the evolution of power in your marriage, business partnership, sibling bond, or mentor-mentee relationship. Often the power exchange in a relationship is hidden and unclear. When the power imbalance is not spoken about openly, it can feel even more disturbing.

Jack and Jill and the Broken Crown

Here is a story: Jill falls madly in love with Jack and is bedazzled by his crown, which promises a fuller and more enriched life. Jill holds Jack in high esteem. He will fill her empty spaces and make up for her deficiencies. Jack loves the feeling of being looked up to and slips into the ascribed role enthusiastically. This arrangement gives him the opportunity to be the hero—just what he wants to be.

Time changes everything. Jill gets a job as a charge nurse, hones her assertiveness skills, and begins to recognize that she is more capable than she knew. At the same time, Jill begins to question how real that crown on Jack's head is. When she reaches for it, Jack fights to keep it on his head. He can't envision life without it. In the ensuing struggle, Jack falls down the hill, loses his crown, and Jill comes tumbling after.

At the bottom of the hill, when they get up and dust themselves off, what happens? Jack bandages his wounds with vinegar and brown paper. (Really, that's how one rendition of the story goes.) But what changes? What's your vinegar and brown paper? How does the rest of your story go? If one of you no longer needs to wear the crown, and the other no longer needs a hero, then each of you has arrived at a healthier balance of power.

Over time, at least one party in a couple usually begins to feel hemmed in or limited in the relational pattern. As identities evolve, the implicit agreements of the past no longer fit. The chafing party aches to try new things. When it comes to finances, how is it that the other party spends money without asking while you feel the need to ask for permission? Or what about the double standard where the other doesn't tell you their whereabouts, and yet they expect you to declare where you've been and where you're going? Perhaps you agitate for more power when you realize that, more times than not, the other party makes the decisions and your wishes are not seriously considered. Situations such as these invite a renegotiation of the power balance, which often results in conflict.

Challenging a relationship's power structure is never easy. Because of the subtle intricacies of power structures, power moves can be difficult to isolate, but you feel them in your gut. Questions can help to expose the power structure as you analyze it after each incident:

- Who takes care of what activities and tasks in your relationship?

- How exactly does the power structure play out between you? (For example, do you fight it, surrender to it, or get power illegitimately in order to shift the balance?)

- What expectations does the other have of you, and what expectations do you have of yourself, that serve to keep the power structure in place?

- Who has more freedom to choose (the where, what, and when of spending money or going on holidays, for instance) and who is disenfranchised?

Initiating a dialogue presents an immediate risk to the power balance, because power is created through language. The words used between two people have a history of meaning that can both empower and disempower. What if one party is highly articulate with words that disarm or put down the other? A dialogue will either maintain the status quo or begin to challenge it. And shifting gears make noise.

Understandably, the person with more power is reluctant to give it up. Since some relational power is based on strength borrowed from the other's weakness, when the disempowered party begins to step into his or her personal power, the originally empowered party feels weaker. Suddenly, the crown-wearer is faced with his or her own sense of insecurity. Fear drives that person to use tactics designed to hold on to power, like discrediting the other or sowing seeds of doubt.

If, until now, you have been the disempowered party, you might feel that the other is resisting you and the renegotiation of power—which they might be. They might also be fighting with you because they are struggling with their own sense of inadequacy. Since the tactics employed are usually acts of fear and desperation, they aren't pretty—anger, scorn, contempt, putdowns, and ultimatums rarely are. Such responses are designed to keep you in your place, because for the person wearing the crown, *no change* is easier than anything else.

If you fail at your legitimate attempts to rebalance power (and quit trying), it is a lose-lose, because once the inequity has been exposed, you cannot erase what you've seen and the situation becomes intolerable. But you are in a dilemma: it's not possible to go back to the way things were, and the other doesn't want you to move forward in the direction that beckons you. If the other can't find a way to surrender to the constructive shifting of power, the rebalancing becomes destructive. Human nature is such that if we can't get power legitimately, we find a way to get it illegitimately. We might withhold information, rail incessantly but take no action, become helpless, shut down intimacy, leverage illness, or withhold forgiveness. This kind of exchange results in both people feeling powerless. Neither of you gets what you really want and you both feel your options closing in on you.

Do we really want more power? Many of us have a precarious relationship with power and powerlessness. If being powerless doesn't sit well with us, why do we choose it at times? Perhaps because if we can claim powerlessness, we can also legitimize inaction—taking control of our life is hard. We can position ourselves one step back from accountability, where we face fewer risks, being more indirect than direct and less responsible rather than more.

If you hold the power, you can use your position as a shield from the other's challenge. Yet there is a cost to this as well, because with the awareness that you are stepping away from the challenge comes the recognition that you're less than you could be.

What keeps a power struggle going? If we are the more powerless one, we are fighting for our sense of self. We believe we need something essential from the other—to feel wanted, validated, approved of or adequate—and the other refuses to give it to us. Ultimately, our continuous trying feeds the power struggle and we never stop feeling deficient in some way.

If you are the other in any of the above scenarios, what stops you from working toward more equality? Likely the answer relates to what you think you would lose from the power shift. Even confusing behavior makes sense at some level. Maybe you fear that if you freely gave credit, your business partner would develop an inflated sense of self and discard you as a partner. Maybe you fear that if you made your spouse a top priority you would be consumed and lose your autonomy. Maybe you think if you really made your sibling/roommate/workmate feel important, they would soak up so much of the limelight that you would be relegated to the shadows.

If you are the partner who wants to equalize power, sometimes your best shot is to renegotiate with yourself rather than with the other. Ask yourself:

- What will you do, and what will you think of yourself, precisely, when you don't get from the other what you want?

- What would it take to go on *despite* the other rather than *because* of them?

- How can you give to yourself what you're not getting from the other?

If you can find a way to answer these questions, then you have broken an unhealthy bond and created opportunity for a healthy rebalancing of power. When you don't get from the other what you need, you have an opportunity to recognize and overcome the patterns that make you give your power away.

Changing Your Tune

"You're Being Defensive," "Don't Take It Personally," "It Wasn't My Intention," "Getting Feedback," and "Power Struggle" are five familiar tunes we play in conflict. Replaying them endlessly maintains the conflict and leaves you stuck. Yet by listening actively to the undertones beneath these refrains—hearing what you have not heard before—you create opportunities to get unstuck. The undertones help you deal with the real fight, enabling you to compose a new tune.

So, What Now?

Five familiar conflict tunes keep playing until you hear and act on the subtleties in their undertones. Seize the moment of tension to learn a catchy, soulful song. Try the following:

- When you find yourself being defensive, try to attend to the part of you that cries for protection, so that you no longer feel the same need to defend yourself from who or what you don't want to be. If you can, describe that vulnerable part in detail. How might you best care for that part of you?

- When you take a comment from the other personally, if you are *making the issue about you* because of your own insecurity, then focus on the other person; if *the problem is about you,* then take one action to rectify it.

- When you hear yourself saying, "It wasn't my intention" (to hurt the other), ask yourself if that is true. If it is not, acknowledge that truth to yourself.

- When you get painful feedback, stay with your confusion and hurt, and take a brave look at what might have merit, and what does not, so that you can act as the person you want to be.

- When you are embroiled in a power struggle—fighting for your sense of self—take one small action that will make you feel better about who you are *right now.* You might, for thirty minutes, consciously stop trying to get attention or approval and instead simply rest in who you are.

CHAPTER 5

Mapping your Conflict Maze

Why bother to map our conflict maze? When we track what's happening between us, we understand ourselves and the other more and have a better chance of changing our course in the conflict journey. Maintaining the fight is the method we use to avoid having the necessary fight with ourselves. We'll now examine how we can use the fight with the other to work through our inner conflict—a worthy challenge. But how do we do it? Since losing our way in conflict is easy, this chapter presents a rudimentary road map with a few signposts to afford us the best chance of staying on track.

When we encounter discouraging detours and untimely roadblocks, such a guide can help us see that delays are to be expected. When we get impatient, it shows us that though the road is long, there are significant stops along the way, and the ultimate destination is worthwhile. This is the outcome of the numerous fights I have tracked throughout thirty years of working with hundreds of people as they find their way through conflict. Though every story is unique, the patterns are similar.

Before we set out, let's first step back to review, with a bird's-eye perspective, the fight with the other. Then we'll explore its various elements in greater detail.

The (Seemingly) Endless Fight

As much as we don't want to fight, some trigger is strong enough to make us come out swinging—either internally or externally. We fight to avert the internal crisis that has been activated by the external conflict. If our pain has been caused by something someone said or did, we might go after them, hoping that they will retract the hurtful things they said or give us the validation we crave. When we don't get what we need from the other, our desperation intensifies. We are also fighting our internal system, because many of our own beliefs, feelings, and fears feed the conflict. For example, we might worry, "Maybe I really *don't* know what I'm talking about," or, "Maybe I *am* a hopeless screw-up."

Since we don't like what we feel, we adopt behaviors that we think will make us feel better. Unfortunately (and understandably), these are mostly defensive behaviors, such as those mentioned in Chapter 3, that inadvertently invite still more pushback from the other. Defenses increase the other's need to make their point and hence intensifies the fight. For example, justifying my behavior might only increase the other's need to show me how I am wrong.

Where to from here? Becoming self-reflective at this juncture will take us further than reflexively focusing on the other. A fight is an opportunity to increase self-awareness. (Note the movement toward increased self-awareness in the diagram below.) Become curious about your reaction and let it lead you to the core of your unease. Who are you struggling not to be? What do you do behaviorally to defend yourself, and how does that sustain the fight?

The Inner Conflict Map below aims to diagram what happens between you and the other—and inside you—during conflict. You will be conscious of some elements while others might well exist in the subconscious—or even unconscious—realm. This map can help you discern where you are at any given moment and choose a course through conflict.

I suggest that you enter the journey at the point that relates to your circumstances. See if you can use the Inner Conflict Map to locate and track your fight. All the signposts are movable. Some might factor in quite large at times and be almost absent at other times. Focus on the place that will help you get traction and move beyond "stuckness." Spend some time examining the conflict map, and then let's explore in more detail each of its signposts.

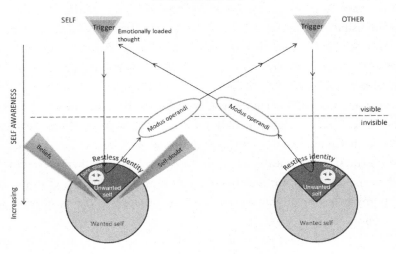

Valuing the Reaction

When your dentist hits a nerve, there is no doubt in either of your minds about what just happened. However, when an emotional nerve gets "hit," the reaction can be much more confusing. Your immediate physical response is clear—muscles tightening, heart rate speeding up, face flushing—but you may not know exactly what's flustering you.

Understanding our own reactions is one of the most significant challenges of conflict, and simultaneously one of the greatest opportunities. If conflict produces a personal reaction that we don't fully understand, then that same conflict has the potential—if we are willing to explore it—to provide a window into who we are. By the same token, if we are genuinely curious about why the conflict triggered such a strong reaction in the other, then we can increase our understanding of that individual, and with it a deeper level of trust and hope in the relationship.

Following the Trigger

We are triggered because something significant within us has been activated. Though we can point to an action or to a word in the *visible zone* of the Inner Conflict Map, the real action takes place in the *invisible zone*—where we feel compelled to protect. Sometimes we are aware of the trigger immediately; other times we only become aware of it after the fact, when we reflect on it: "Wait a minute. What did he say? How *could* he?" On another occasion, the slow accumulation of slights, inferences, or destructive patterns might finally set us off. The trigger might simply be "a look."

The trigger spurs a reaction because we experience it as a threat. Although we can't always immediately or directly connect the threat to our identity, we feel we've been affronted in some way. If we think that what the other said or did reflects negatively on who we are, we're likely to feel angry, humiliated, or frightened, to name a few responses. The offending action demands attention.

Sometimes we rail against the affront and other times we simply take note. The difference has to do with how comfortable we are with ourselves. If there is a slight to our identity and we are reasonably okay with the trait highlighted, we won't be undone by it. If, on the other hand, we struggle, consciously or unconsciously, with this tendency, we're likely to react with strong emotion. When Jamie accuses Justine of being judgmental, she goes into full defense mode, attempting to prove how nonjudgmental she is, because she doesn't *want* to be judgmental—and yet, she is.

Examining the Emotionally Loaded Thought

You'll notice on the Inner Conflict Map that the emotionally loaded thought (represented by the lighter triangle) surrounds the trigger. In fact, it functions as a lens through which we view the trigger. After all, only our interpretation converts a stimulus into a trigger. If we experience the stimulus to be a threat to self, then it becomes a trigger, and a reaction ensues. Such a response may be uniquely our own, or others may also find the stimulus problematic. If we are the only one who becomes reactive, then we know it's time to reflect on ourselves or on our dynamic with the person who triggered us.

Though the emotionally loaded thought contains both a *thought* and a *feeling*, we might not be able to name them. We might simply see red and know something big has taken hold. Response to the trigger happens so quickly that we might find it hard to analyze the reaction's components. Or we might be able to name the feeling generated by the thought. Some people find it easier to name the feeling than the thought that comes before it.

When the trigger tugs at our identity, even if we can name the feelings, we don't hold those feelings long because doing so is too much for the moment. The primary feelings, like hurt or sadness, make us too vulnerable. To get away from them we focus on the other, becoming incensed by what was said or done. This secondary feeling of anger is easier to tolerate, because at least it makes us feel a little stronger. Becoming aware of our emotionally loaded thought enables us to more effectively challenge it.

Caring for Your Sore Spot

The trigger hits a nerve: a sore spot that resides in the wounded and restless part of our identity. This tender and bruised part holds the residual pain we have collected thus far in our life. Often this is old pain that took root in childhood, but it might also be newer. These sore spots form when we are left weakened or helpless by the behavior of a significant someone. The hurt creates an enduring vulnerability that makes us sensitive to a similar pain being reactivated in a current relationship: a cycle, in which the other activates our pain and we try to protect ourselves from more, quickly ensues.

Though—in the attempt to avoid the pain—the sore spot can drive the cycle, it might be quite removed from the trigger. For instance, your sore spot might have to do with being rejected as a teenager, and yet the trigger might be that your adult lover isn't thrilled with the gift you gave her. Making the connection between the trigger and the sore spot can be difficult. This sore spot is not something we likely spend much time thinking about, and we might not be able to describe it. In fact, if someone were to ask what was bothering us in a conflict situation, we would respond with something quite different than the sore spot. We would refer to something concrete and specific, visible in the immediate interaction.

Yet maybe what we think we're agitated about is not what's upsetting us the most. The offensive behavior or uncomfortable feeling is easier to peg than precisely what is undoing us. On the Inner Conflict Map, the most important matters are taking place in the *invisible zone*, which we often cannot easily access. The sore spot usually lies dormant, unless it's poked.

The trigger may have activated the sore spot as well as the "unwanted self"; both exist in the restless part of our identity, in the invisible zone, where we feel most vulnerable. The sore spot and the aspects of self we deny might feel indistinguishable. But the sore spot aches for the kind of tender loving care that will ultimately heal the sensitivity.

Accessing Your Unwanted Self

The unwanted self is one of two people: the person you don't want to be and yet fear that you might be; or, in contrast, the person you would like to be and are afraid that you're not. When you try to name the unwanted self, don't overthink. Instead notice the comment from the other that really gets to you and sticks. Then focus on what you think the comment says about you. For example, Mandy says to Hillary, "I knew we had to make sure to have the right chardonnay because you were coming." Hillary realizes she's taken the comment to be one more dig about being "high maintenance"—what she doesn't want to be.

You might become aware of the unwanted self at the level of behavior and what it says about who you are. For example, "I am controlling and therefore I am an ogre." You might be very aware of who you don't want to be, but secretly fear that you are exactly that; you don't want to be incompetent, undisciplined, unreliable, a failure, too critical, or too demanding—and yet sometimes you are. Or you would like to be generous, forgiving, in control, wise, or loving—and sometimes you're not. Sometimes the unwanted self is who you become when you are running from the sore spot. You don't like it, but you don't know another way to shield yourself from the pain. So, you lash out, stonewall, become condescending, or grab the limelight. Here, the unwanted self is what limits you. In tandem, the sore spot and the unwanted self drive the conflict cycle.

Note: You might or might not be able to identify your unwanted self. If you can't, simply wondering about it now might encourage your noticing it when it operates in the interaction between you and the other. Even if you can put words to it, you might realize that there is something behind it that is even more core. The unwanted self is the transformative part of yourself that cries out to be dealt with.

Defaulting to Your M.O.

We all adopt characteristic methods of fleeing from pain. If the term "modus operandi," or M.O., seems like a strange term to use in this context, think about how police use it. Police refer to modus operandi when they're looking for a criminal's distinct pattern of behavior, or in criminal profiling when they search for clues to an offender's psychology. I'm not saying we're criminals, but we do have habitual ways of behaving.

At times, my clients refer to their opponent's M.O.—they know what to expect from the other because they have witnessed their patterns. Falling into automated ways of doing something is particularly common during stressful times. Looking at what we do while in emotional pain reveals our modus operandi. As you can see on the Inner Conflict Map, our M.O.s cross the line from the invisible to the visible, from the territory of psychological mindsets to the world of behaviors.

Your habit in times of conflict might be to step forward or backward, to attack or withdraw, to operate overtly or more covertly. You might combine methods or flip back and forth, which can be confusing to the other.

When you don't want to be excluded, dismissed, or rejected, do you step forward, redoubling your efforts, or do you step back, hoping that someone will reach out to you? Deciphering the difference between attacking and withdrawing is not always simple. Though passive-aggressive behavior doesn't look like an attack on the surface, it is nonetheless a sneaky, indirect strike. For example, I am agreeable and smile at my manager, but I deliberately undermine her, neglecting to deliver what she needs to be effective—and I give her a lame excuse about why I didn't come through. Controlling behavior can be blatant or take subtle, covert forms, including charming persuasion, disarming manipulation, or cold silence. Perhaps you made mental commitments to yourself—I will not be at fault, I will not be seen as weak, or I will not be told what to do—and they propel your behavioral patterns.

Though some behaviors may be troublesome, we don't necessarily intend to cause trouble. We simply adopt a course of action we believe will make us feel better and fend off greater pain. When one method proves to be unsuccessful, we might switch to another. For example, at the outset, I might attempt to pacify or plead, and when that doesn't produce the results I hoped for, I might resort to a more aggressive approach. We (mostly subconsciously) choose our modus operandi to protect our vulnerabilities, and unfortunately the pain remains because the opportunity for healing is misspent.

Cherisse and Ahmed: Mapping Their Conflict Maze

Cherisse thinks a holiday Monday with pelting rain is the perfect time to paint the kids' room. She checks with her husband, Ahmed, and he agrees to the joint project. When it's time to begin and her husband is missing in action, Cherisse traipses off to the den, and sure enough, there he is with his eyes glued to the computer screen. She wonders, "What's he up to this time?"

"I'll be there in a minute," he says. "I've got just a couple of work items that need to be knocked off."

Cherisse feels her blood pressure soar and her heart pound with anger. There is always something more important than her priorities. "Last Saturday when I needed you here, you were helping the neighbors again," she points out. "When *they* need something, the willing guy hops right to it," she says sarcastically.

Ouch. Ahmed feels the criticism. He has screwed up again. He must do something to right matters between them because he can't stand feeling like a jerk. He tries to explain: "The boss is waiting for these few items. I'm under some real pressure here."

"Well there's always something isn't there?" Cherisse mutters quietly.

Ahmed sees her look, realizes that his explanation doesn't suffice, and promises to do better next time. Inwardly he knows he wastes too much time surfing the net for cars.

Cherisse gives a half-hearted nod. Inside Ahmed thinks, "This woman is impossible to please." He switches tactics, deciding to look out for himself instead.

What is happening within each and between them? Here's a typical scenario:

- Cherisse is *triggered* by seeing Ahmed at the computer—again. She interprets that stimulus to mean that she is not a priority and there-fore not important (*emotionally loaded thought*). The *anger feeling* is instantaneous and is fuelled by her *belief* that there is always some-thing more important than her.

- Cherisse concludes that, once again, her wants have been dismissed. Her husband's behavior hits a *sore spot*. Cherisse often felt overlooked by her father, who favored her younger sister. It's a vulnerability she carries with her.

- Cherisse is determined that she cannot and will not endure the pain of invisibility in her adult life. She determines that she will be noticed, and to accomplish that she reminds Ahmed of the other times when he has failed to be there for her: her M.O. is evident. She believes that keeping the pressure on him is her best chance of getting what she needs.

- Meanwhile, Ahmed is *triggered* by Cherisse's tone and look, even more so than by her words. His *emotionally loaded thought* is: "I've screwed up again." She is obviously unhappy with him, which makes him feel unaccepted by her and unacceptable. Her attack hits a *sore spot*.

- Ahmed taps ever so briefly into a previously subconscious memory: as a child he longed for his mother's affection, but she paid more attention to her career. Affection is what he now longs for from Cherisse, and once again it seems just out of reach.

- To run from the pain of feeling unlovable, Ahmed falls to his M.O.—to get acceptance and avoid rejection—and becomes a pleaser. He overdoes it: he apologizes to stop the complaints, and he promises too much, trying to create hope. He attempts to get out of trouble, but the trouble continues because some words rings hollow.

- Cherisse resorts to familiar habits. She lets Ahmed know in what ways he doesn't meet her expectations.

- This behavior merely fuels Ahmed's belief that Cherisse really cannot be pleased and that she will continue to be critical and demanding. Therefore, he switches to a new M.O.: he retreats to protect himself, becoming unavailable to Cherisse.

- Cherisse begins to feel that Ahmed is hurting her deliberately—and he might be. Or he might simply be running from the feeling of being unacceptable, and such behavior is hurtful to Cherisse. Either way, there is more going on: since Ahmed doesn't want to feel like a failure (his unwanted self), he puts Cherisse on the back burner. He becomes passive-aggressive with his looks, which are both contemptuous and controlling. He will not let Cherisse come close.

- Her anxiety is rising because none of her methods is getting her needs met. Cherisse feels increasingly helpless. She attempts to regain some power by deciding she's done with the relationship.

- Both are at a loss about what to do next. Cherisse *doubts* herself. She fears that Ahmed will leave because she isn't good enough for him. She wonders if she has what it takes to live on her own. Cherisse doesn't want to be critical or demanding; she's just desperate not to be overlooked. She doesn't want to be unimportant (her unwanted self); she longs to be cherished and loved well.

- At the same time, Ahmed *doubts* his ability to be a successful partner because he isn't getting it right. He doesn't want to be inadequate and unlovable (his unwanted self), yet his behavior, at times, makes him this way.

Cherisse and Ahmed are caught up in a sticky, intricate, and complicated web of interactions. Each response takes them further away from what they really want and who they want to be. Underneath the pain is a warm, radiant, and expressive Cherisse who longs for deep connection with Ahmed. Ahmed's heart, meanwhile, is unusually responsive to others, investing willingly and generously. He longs to enjoy and be enjoyed by his wife. They have all the necessary ingredients for a loving, vibrant relationship, and yet they get fouled up.

Cherisse is determined that Ahmed must satisfy her need to be seen and cherished. Ahmed believes that to feel adequate and acceptable, he must meet Cherisse's needs, yet he also believes that her needs are greater than he can fill. It's complicated for Cherisse as well. Ahmed seems to need some nudging to be attentive, so sometimes pursuing attention works for her—but not always.

A question remains: how much should they depend on each other to get their needs met, and at what point does their dynamic keep them stuck?

An Endless Game

When, during conflict, you and the other both engage your modus operandi to protect your uncomfortable, painful place, the tossing back and forth can feel like a desperate game of ping-pong. The game for both sides goes something like this:

Objective: Stay away from your painful place.

Strategy:

- Keep the volleying going for as long as you can, because it prevents you from the discomfort of looking at yourself.

- Keep the focus on your opponent as the problem.

- Drive the interactions with your modus operandi.

- Defend and protect yourself at all cost.

- If there is a negative focus on you, don't let it stick and revert focus to the other.

- If you are implicated negatively and it sticks, justify your actions.

- Make inferences and attributions about the other's identity ("He's basically selfish,") and don't allow yours to be challenged ("Me, critical? That's ridiculous!").

- Sacrifice self-awareness for temporarily increased comfort.

Rules:

- Anything goes and you can play as dirty as you like, because there is no referee.

- End the game when one of you tires sufficiently to quit.

- Pick up where you left off on another day. (Some people have been known to keep the game going for practically a lifetime.)

Winners and losers. The intrigue of the game is partly because it's ambiguous—who wins and who loses? Some would say there are only losers. But if that were the case, the game would stop. Staying out of the uncomfortable zone in which self-awareness increases feels like a win, at least in the short run.

The discouraging and frustrating conflict game keeps us hooked for too long. On the Inner Conflict Map, we can get stuck at the trigger, the emotionally loaded thought, the sore spot, the unwanted self, or the modus operandi. Conversely, we can use any one of these signposts to move in a different direction. In the next chapter, we'll further explore the cycle trap, because although we may want to extricate ourselves from wearisome conflict cycles, we could be feeding them at the same time. Once we understand where we get trapped, we can create the change we crave.

So, What Now?

Think of a recent, significant conflict and begin to fill in the Inner Conflict Map. Use the diagram to track what's happening between you and the other, and what's happening inside you, during a fight. This is an opportunity to zoom in on your conflict maze and see it in a broader context. Consider the following:

- How did your interpretation of the stimulus convert it into a trigger, threatening your self-identity?

- Can you put what you feel into words?

- How do you habitually behave when you feel those feelings?

- Who do you *not* want to be?

- For now, do nothing but look at the bigger picture to see how it fits together.

CHAPTER 6

Getting Out of the Cycle Trap

I was caught in a vicious cycle in my marriage for years. The cycle often took us to the same place, where we stalled. I would raise an issue and inevitably my husband, Diet, would say something that I would take to mean that I was a "pill," or a malcontent. Why couldn't I just be happy with the way things were? Why did I have to once again raise an issue? Necessary questions, but they also made me doubt myself. I didn't want to be the unlovable malcontent, so the thought that I might be was just enough to make me back down, and the cycle stalled.

Meanwhile, Diet didn't want to be the "bad guy" who wasn't measuring up and avoided that by being critical of me, in mostly non-verbal ways—a disapproving look or disgruntled sigh. But it would be only a matter of time before another trigger activated the familiar cycle, and we would be back at the same place. And as much as I didn't want to raise issues, another compelling one would be staring me in the face. If I didn't address it, I would feel like something had come between us and I would lose my warmth. I was stuck.

Virtuous and vicious cycles are common concepts in the fields of environment, economics, business, management, and psychology, to name a few. A cycle exists when a continuous chain of events is self-reinforcing. Virtuous cycles obviously produce positive outcomes, while vicious cycles produce negative ones. "Vicious" sounds like a severe term in the context of conflict, but I use the term because it simply references a detrimental outcome and is understandable across a variety of disciplines.

Being stuck in a vicious cycle of conflict is enormously frustrating because we can't find a way out—and worse yet we perpetuate the cycle. Although we didn't reach a good result in our previous argument, we have another to address a similar issue, with only a faint hope of securing a better outcome this time. People leave relationships—or remain dissatisfied within them—when they have lost hope that they can break this vicious cycle. Hence exploring the cycle trap and tracking the negative self-reinforcement is essential to shifting from a vicious cycle to a virtuous one.

When the cycle solves one problem (for example, it addresses my unrest related to an issue) while creating another chronic issue (I feel like an unlovable malcontent, for instance), it's a cycle trap. In the case of my marriage, in the short term, if I focused blame on Diet for what he or his body said to me, then I didn't have to face the inner turmoil that his words or actions activated. Yet when I blamed him so that I could protect my vulnerable, restless self, he pushed back. The longer this pattern kept going, the longer pain remained, and only intensified when I tried to get away from it. Below you'll find a diagram of my Inner Conflict Cycle, which is based on the Inner Conflict Map in Chapter 5.

Meanwhile, here is a breakdown of how vicious cycles are reinforced:

- You get triggered, and you refuse to stay where the trigger takes you because of the pain caused by what you think it says about who you are. (In my story, I was an unlovable malcontent.)

- Your habitual modus operandi (M.O.) then takes you as far away as possible from the sore spot or unwanted self that were triggered in your restless identity. (Personally, I blamed Diet and justified myself to deny that I was the problem.)

- Your unique defense pattern triggers the other's sore spot or unwanted self. (In my story, Diet didn't want to be the "bad one" who didn't measure up.)

- The other falls to their M.O. to avoid their uncomfortable place. (In our story, Diet criticized me in subtle ways.) Their distinct behavioral pattern triggers your restless identity. (Once again, I felt like I was the problem.)

- Each of you is simply trying to take care of yourself by running from the uncomfortable place, but because you are the perfect match, what you do when you run pushes the other back to the uncomfortable parts of themselves.

- Therefore, you must fight the other and they must fight you. The cycle is perfectly self-reinforcing and can sustain itself for years.

When you track what's happening within you and between you, it's easy to visualize how the cycle becomes self-reinforcing. The other's trigger activates your identity issue at the lower level, which then drives your distinct defensive behavioral pattern (M.O.), seen higher up on the diagram. Your defensive behavior triggers the other's restless identity, which then drives their defensive behavior. Tracing the arrows, you can see how they create a perfect self-reinforcing loop. Along with the diagram that maps the conflict between me and Diet, below is a diagram for you to fill in. It contains two important questions for your self-reflection: What do you do to defend yourself, and Who do you not want to be?

MY INNER CONFLICT CYCLE

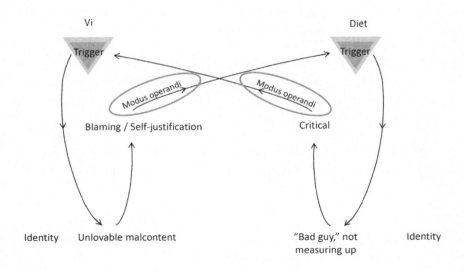

Your cycle. When you fill in the map with your own cycle, try to capture the specific terms unique to your dance. M.O.s often involve withdrawing or attacking (moving away or toward). The restless identity usually wants to feel either significant or secure—it's what is threatened and what you feel the need to protect. Work with it until you find the words that resonate with your distinct experience.

INNER CONFLICT CYCLE

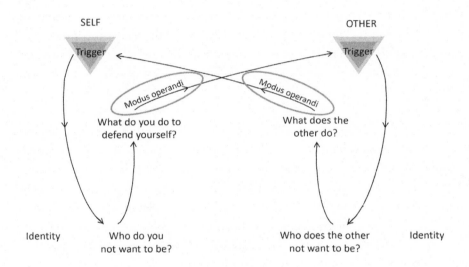

As you track the cycle, you'll recognize that's reason for hope, because if you choose to deal with the unwanted self and sore spot instead of running away, you can shift from a vicious to a virtuous cycle. Or if you choose to do something other than your M.O., the cycle can no longer be the same. You're no longer feeding it.

What Makes Cycles Hard to Break?

Though there's good reason to hope, we also know that interrupting vicious cycles presents a significant challenge. We stay stuck because the obstacles are considerable—including our own self-doubt, our beliefs, and the other's tendency when we adopt a new behavior to up the ante in conflict. Let's consider each of these factors in more detail.

Self-doubt can be your weakest link. In the cycle, the other hits you in a sensitive place. Perhaps you doubt your capabilities or character. Though you started out strong and clear in addressing an issue, you succumb once more to fear and lose your power. The other may have been manipulative, excessively cruel, judgmental, empathetic, or persuasive. Whatever they've done or said, you can no longer see clearly; you're disoriented and floundering. Your confidence has been considerably reduced. Or perhaps you recognize that the other is right about you, and only when you accept the indictment and try to change can you extract yourself from the cycle. Wrestling with and working through, or "wrestling through," this moment of self-doubt changes everything.

Beliefs fuel your feelings and behavior. Your beliefs underpin every interaction. They are deeply rooted and highly resistant to change, unlike feelings, which respond rapidly to their immediate environment. Your beliefs are the interim conclusions that you have derived from all your life's experiences. They help you make sense of what is. Since beliefs are a resting place for you, you will be reluctant if someone tries to unseat them. Even if you allow them to be challenged briefly, you quickly revert to your deeply ingrained thinking patterns.

Disempowering self-beliefs tend to be particularly entrenched. Here are some examples:

- "I am too much." (—too dramatic, too detailed, or too certain.)

- "I can't show weakness."

- "I'm uninteresting."

Beliefs you have about the world may have crept in ever so subtly and be hard to shake. Consider these examples:

- "Marriage is an implied consent to be controlled."

- "Men only think about themselves."

- "Women can't be satisfied."

Such embedded beliefs perpetuate the vicious cycle because, with Ole Iggy dominating, the rational brain can't have sufficient impact. Yet if you could calm Iggy, you could question the belief that holds you back. A disorienting moment contains the possibility of surmounting your limitation. Otherwise, your stubborn beliefs leave you trapped in the cycle you want to escape.

The other ups the ante. While in conflict, if you try something different than falling into familiar patterns your discomfort will only increase, because the other will up the ante, doing more of what worked before—or unveiling a new tactic. For example, if your tendency is to comply and instead you assert yourself, the other will likely apply more pressure. They might plead, persuade, manipulate, become nasty, threaten to leave a relationship, or even commit suicide. Upping the ante can go from mild to severe forms of behavior. To get out of this vicious cycle requires increasing your tolerance for discomfort.

What is the Tragedy of Vicious Cycles?

Good people who engage each other with concerted and sincere efforts often end up not only stuck but also, unfortunately, in a worse place—and that is heartbreaking. Why are vicious cycles tragic? Because:

- *Being stuck in endless vicious cycles feels futile.* Considerable time, energy, and angst are expended on a troubling issue, with little return on your investment. You travel so far, only to realize you've gone nowhere. You abandon the interaction, not because you're satisfied with the outcome but because you are too drained to continue.

- *The critical issue remains.* When you succumb to powerlessness, the legitimate issue that needs to be addressed between you and the other gets lost in the cycle. Yet whatever you are fighting about is too compelling to be ignored. Thus it drags you into another round, despite your dread of the looming cycle, despite failed attempts to work though the issues, and despite your skepticism about a successful outcome this time.

- *Failure to work through the critical issue entrenches it.* When you're caught in a vicious cycle and don't take the opportunity to address the critical issue, it gets fortified. This costly experience makes you only more determined to safeguard yourself. You already know the well-worn track the other is on—where they will poke away at you—and you don't want to subject yourself to that one more time. It is as if you build up an allergy to the other.

Deconstructing Your Vicious Cycle

Take a moment to reflect on an enduring conflict you're in, one in which you experience a sensation of déjà vu—that you've been at the same place in the argument many times before. Use the six questions below to identify your vicious cycle's components, which present opportunities to make the cycle a virtuous one.

What is the trigger that set you off? It might be what the other has said—something immediate and in your face—or a frustration may have been building inside for quite some time, until a situation becomes too much and you can't contain your reaction. In this case, the trigger might appear insignificant to everyone but you. During a fight, you might be set off by numerous triggers, activating more than one M.O. Suddenly there's something more to protect.

What is the emotionally loaded thought that surrounds the trigger? As discussed earlier, the trigger is about how you interpret a stimulus. But this interpretation happens mostly automatically, so identifying it might require some reflection. The emotionally loaded thought usually has an uncomfortable implication for your identity. What's the thought that comes *right before* the potent *feeling*? If you can't name the thought, can you name the feeling? In conflict, you might simply kick into a behavioral response that takes you away from a feeling you don't like. Either during conflict or following it, taking time to understand your thoughts and feelings is important, because they affect your behavior.

What sore spot or nerve has been hit? Your sore spot is connected to your vulnerability. It's your "ouch" factor.

What is your unwanted self? What is the self that you don't want to be? Pay attention to the self that makes you squirm and holds you back. It might also be the (unwanted) self that you become when you try to protect yourself from pain.

What is your modus operandi? What behavioral and thought patterns do you enact when you're running from emotional pain? Do you step forward or step back, attack or withdraw? What are you fighting for? You might want to be part of the game, to have your contribution acknowledged, to avoid being dismissed, or something else. Your distinct pattern is defensive and wants to achieve that goal.

When do you lose power? Is it when you cave in to self-doubt or is it when you bump up against who you don't want to be (your unwanted self)?

Deconstructing the Other's Vicious Cycle

Deconstructing your own cycle is challenging enough, but can you also become curious about what's happening for the other? Don't do this to analyze them but rather to empathize with them and to expand your understanding of what it might be like to be them. The other's process is like yours but there will be differences.

What might be the other's trigger? Think about what is really going on with you in relation to the other. What actions or words might have offended them?

What emotionally loaded thought might surround the other's trigger? What do you know about the other's predominant thinking patterns and how those link to their view of self? How does the other usually express their feelings? What cues do you look for to know what they're feeling? Feelings might be expressed outwardly, inwardly, blatantly, or furtively—so they can be hard to read. When it comes to anger, for instance, one person might express it outwardly. Another person might hold anger close and then unleash passive-aggressively. Someone else might smile, say everything's copasetic, and then let their real feelings rip with a third party.

What might be the other's sore spot? Have you witnessed any patterns in previous conflict situations? What do they tend to get sensitive or heated around?

What might be the other's unwanted self? Who are they fighting not to be? You might know better than them, precisely because they work so hard not to see that aspect of themselves.

What might be the other's modus operandi? Because the other's distinct behavioral patterns impact you, you probably know them well. For example, you see how the other undermines you to quell their feelings of insecurity; you feel the sting of underhanded digs when the other's buried sense of inadequacy takes control.

When does the other lose power? For a personal victory, do you target the other's weakest link (for example, self-doubt)? At what point does the other cave?

The Way Out

Every conflict presents several ways out. In the middle of a conflict cycle, taking a temporary escape route can be tempting when you don't have the wherewithal to see a round through. That is the reality—sometimes it just feels too hard. You take the back door, and perhaps you'll re-engage at another time.

An alternative option is to face yourself in a new way. You can examine your behavior—the distinct pattern—and after you acknowledge its hurtful impact on the other, commit yourself to changing it by taking one little step. You might deal directly with what causes discomfort in your restless identity—the sore spot or unwanted self. Taking this route stopped the vicious cycle in my marriage: I faced the fact that I *could* be a malcontent, and I learned to address issues and be lovable at the same time.

This alternative option presents a substantial challenge, because it asks you to open yourself up when you feel threatened. A saving grace, however, is that you open up to *yourself* first. The most important relationship at this juncture is with yourself. This is deeply spiritual work. You ask, "Who am I and who do I want to be?" As you shift the focus inward, what's happening with the other becomes almost inconsequential. If you have the stamina and heart to face what you've been running from—to stay with the challenge to self that the other has highlighted for you—then you can free yourself from the cycle trap, *regardless of what the other does*. In Part 3, we'll consider in depth the process of going within to have the fight with yourself.

So, What Now?

When you face your unwanted self rather than run from it, you are more able to address the problem between you and the other. Take the first steps to starve the vicious cycle:

- Using the Inner Conflict Cycle, plot your own behaviors and the identity struggle triggered by the other.

- Fill in as much as you can for the other as well. Their behavior might be clearer than their identity struggle.

- Follow the arrows and notice how your behavior triggers the restless identity of the other. Consider the self-reinforcing loop between you.

- Choose one way to change. By behaving differently or acknowledging your identity struggle, you can shift from the vicious to the virtuous cycle. Fortunately, it only takes one person to interrupt the cycle.

PART 3
EMBRACING THE FIGHT WITHIN

Embracing self means lovingly taking care of the part that limits you (and gets you into trouble with others). By working through the difference between who you are and who you want to be, you integrate all your parts and become more comfortable with yourself, learning to like yourself more.

CHAPTER 7

Peeling Back Inner Disturbance

Georgia's been up half the night worrying about a critical board meeting. She tries to look self-assured when she enters the board room, but even her strategically worn favorite blue shirt/gray suit combo doesn't conceal her hangdog spirit. Board members have not been happy with her performance, and they're making decisions about her future as leader of the marketing company. When they ask her tough questions, Georgia fronts with a calm demeanour—she has a "fake it till you make it" mentality. "We've implemented some important initiatives and right now we just need a little more time," she says. She can't afford to be vulnerable. But she acquiesces, flips back and forth, and sometimes remains silent, cracks appearing in her outer shell, and it becomes evident that Georgia doesn't have the answers. She defends herself by saying, "You don't really understand my understated, collaborative leadership style," and secretly believes that at least one or two of the board members have it out for her. One member responds, "Numbers don't lie. If this weren't a family business, you would have been gone a long time ago."

What's the problem for Georgia? She hasn't really faced her sense of inadequacy in her role—her unwanted self. But doing so is difficult. She has expectations for herself, she believes her parents have expectations for her, and she is painfully aware of the board members' expectations of her. What's the cost of not acknowledging her feelings of inadequacy? She's forced to keep putting energy into her persona—playing the part—yet her inner turmoil continues. She feels unsuccessful, and the external conflict between her and the board intensifies.

The various happenings in our external world can trigger an internal struggle between *who we are* and *who we think we need to be for the other*. Expectations both propel and inform the difference between the two. The expectations we place on ourselves relate to what we deem important; they reflect our understanding about who we need to be in this world—which is also influenced by others' expectations of us. Though the incongruence between these two doesn't feel good, it creates a pregnant tension that potentially births a greater sense of alignment inside and out—with an increased sense of peace.

Identity, or who we are, is important because it shapes our experience of effectiveness in the world. The perception that we've hit the mark instead of missed it begets a sense of success, and happiness. Yet the struggle amongst the varying parts of ourselves often holds us back—it's an identity clash.

The Internal Identity Clash

Using the diagram of an onion whose layers can be peeled back helps in visualizing the identity clash within. It allows us to consider our various selves in the diverse contexts in which they're shaped and manifested. The interplay between the outer circles and the evolving self at the core provides the stimulus for change.

ONION SKIN IDENTITY MODEL:
Who I am and Who I Need to Be for the Other

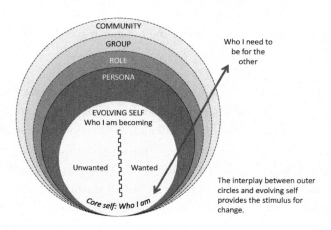

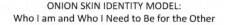

71

The different layers of identity depicted in the diagram can easily fight with each other rather than be in alignment. Who you think you need to be in the community may oppose who you think you really are at your core. Or perhaps who you think you need to be in the groups you haven't chosen—like your family, gender, or ethnicity—doesn't fit with who you think you are. Or who you think you need to be in the various roles you fill may not fit with the essence of you. To overcome the dissonance, you take on a persona and become *who you think you need to be for the other* in a particular context. Though the persona runs through all four layers, evidenced by the shading in the diagram, a specific layer devoted to the persona highlights its strong connection to the core self.

Even at your core, a struggle exists between the self you don't want to be (and believe you are) and the self you want to be (and aren't yet), which is, fortunately, the state of an evolving self. What you do with the incongruence between the various parts of yourself forms your identity. Because of its potential for propelling personal growth, we'll focus on incongruence throughout this chapter. We'll examine each part of the onion more specifically, starting with communities.

Your communities. The outer onion identity layer is community, which can include any organizational context. To reflect on the congruence between who you are in community you can ask, "Do the values of my community fit with my own?"; "Do I feel like I need to be more conservative, more colorful, more informed, more experienced, or wealthier?" At each layer of the onion, the question remains, Will you ignore the incongruence, dismiss it, or use it for change?

Groups you find yourself in. Groups you don't choose represent a particularly poignant struggle between *who you are* and *who you think you need to be*, because there is no easy exit. Do the culturally ascribed characteristics of your gender align with who you are? Who do you think you need to be for acceptance? What if you can't relate to the ethnic or religious group or nationality you were born into? Family is another unchosen grouping, and a particularly impactful one because of our inbuilt need for belonging. Fellow group members' expectations and the lives they lead will affect who you think you need to be and your determining how you'll be different or the same. Each group has its own identity, and you fit to varying degrees. You also assume an identity from these important reference groups.

Roles you fill. In the various roles you fill, how does *who you are* fit with *who you think you need to be*? At work, the external demands of your role may bump up against your expectation of who you need to be. What is your belief about your capacity to perform? If you don't think you have what it takes, then internal disturbance is the result. Do the role and the company culture fit with who you are, or do you feel like you must take on too much in that position or environment that is not and never will be you?

In some roles you have a choice, and in others you don't. Though you might feel that the parental role doesn't fit you, you can't be excused from it. What is the congruence between *who you are* and *who you think you need to be* as a partner? Your partner's feedback informs and likely increases any dissonance here. If you seriously consider the feedback rather than dismiss it, you might be more disturbed in the short run but less so in the long run because your relationship will be improved. On yet another front, what is the fit like between *who you are* as a child to your parent(s) and *who you think you should be*? Experiencing incongruence in familial roles can be particularly profound because the stakes are high. Stress is greatest when you feel you can't perform an expected role but still need to, or don't want to and believe you should.

Function of the persona. Adopting a persona is a common way to bridge the gap between *who we are* and *who we think we need to be*. Putting energy into the persona is purposeful (though often unconscious). We are just trying to "get it right"—to be more effective. Persona is the projection of what we expect from ourselves in a context. It's also influenced by others' expectations of us. It is our understanding of the way we need to be for the other. Yet if we're pretending to be someone we're not, we're minimizing and betraying who we are. Meanwhile, dropping the persona feels risky, because doing so can make us feel like we'll lose control of how we'll be perceived. Image making feels a little safer. Persona is our interpretation of who we need to be, to be acceptable. To let go of that can feel chaotic.

Addressing the incongruence between the parts of our identity is important because it helps us better understand our inner conflict. If we better understand our inner conflict, we will be more equipped to work through our conflict with others.

Benefits of the Incongruence, or "Non-fit"
A running theme in this book is that discomfort—in this case from internal incongruence—brings benefits. By confronting our discomfort, we can begin to recognize our inner conflict and move toward inner peace and less external conflict. Let's explore four potential benefits of incongruence.

Provides the energy for change. Because the experience of incongruence is disturbing, it provides the energy for personal change. It's hard to change on our own, so we often grow personally in the context of relationship. Relational conflict potentially drives a deeper journey into self, and inner conflict drives the profundity of relationship. Understanding the connection between the external and internal fight makes it possible for us to change ourselves and therefore our relationships. Either we use the energy for change or we shut it down.

Highlights who we are. The incongruence, or non-fit, between *who we think we are* and *who we think we need to be* gives us an awareness of self and highlights who we *actually* are. Identity is not something we usually think much about because it's just "who we are." Then some conflict triggers an awareness of our identity, particularly if we can shift from the reactive reptilian brain to the neocortex. Initially we don't even know that we are fighting our own identity. We only know that we're uncomfortable. We don't readily connect our discomfort to something deeper because we're just being *who we are* in our given environment. We don't automatically turn the gaze on ourselves when we're in conflict with the other because we don't think our reactions are unique. We think that anyone would respond the way we do, given the same situation.

Usually we're not even aware of the difference between who we really are and the persona we project. We become aware of identity when something alters the way we view ourselves. Conflict triggers the incongruence of our identity. Yet when another person is acting out their persona, we *can* feel it. He walks away and we can't help but think, "He's full of it." We can see right through the words or actions because they don't feel authentic. Or she is so carefully crafted, we just want to give her a shake and tell her to be herself, because her striving to be something other than she is creates a barrier. Being unclear within about what is core self and what is persona creates the stress of uncertainty. Uncertainty, in turn, gives rise to the question, "Who am I, really?" which points to another question: "Who do I want to be?" This question signals the potential for change.

Brings us to core self. The incongruence within and between the various layers of identity shown in the onion diagram is brought back to the core self in the center—and nestled in there are the wanted and unwanted selves (see Chapter 5). We probably already like many parts of ourselves. We also have a picture of what we can be. The unwanted self contains some of the pain we have collected so far in life and acts in response to it. The world shouts at us—telling us who we are and who we ought to be. In our families, we learn whether we're listened to or noticed, whether we talk too much or not enough, if we are viewed as being happy, stubborn, reliable, an achiever or an underachiever. Incident by incident our identity takes shape in a context that places us in dynamic interaction with a sometimes nurturing and sometimes hostile environment, telling us what we are and are not. A constant inner struggle determines which of these messages we'll accept and integrate into *who we think we are* and *who we think we need to be* to exist in this world. Not every message has the same effect. Each will be compared with other messages about who we are.

A negative message has maximum impact when it hits us at a particularly vulnerable time, when we feel weakened for whatever reason—possibly in a new setting, at a new stage of development, or when we lack support. Then, this restless, tender part of our identity is tempted to agree. Often the negative message comes from a person of influence, which makes it even harder to refute. Throw in some public humiliation, and shame ripples out from the weight of the stone.

Painful messages about who we are obstruct change, because emotionally loaded thoughts carry a strong link to the primitive brain. Ole Iggy comes to our rescue, and the fight-or-flight response takes over rather than employing our rational brain to process the hurtful, self-limiting beliefs. These beliefs shape a negative identity and we then perceive the environment through that filter.

Leverages an evolving self. Identity incongruence is a potent force in leveraging an evolving self. However, incongruence works both for and against change—either we use the discomfort to propel change, or we dismiss it because it's too unsettling. Keeping in mind the onion skin diagram, let yourself feel the tension between the various parts of yourself that the layers depict; if you are too uncomfortable with the tension between the parts, you may be tempted to jettison one rather than working with the incongruence toward an integrated healthy self-identity.

What to Do with Incongruence

If you become aware of incongruence between any of the layers of your identity, the question is, Will you use the incongruence between *who you are* and *who you think you need to be* for personal change or not? Here are three scenarios that could occur when you become aware of incongruence:

- If you don't acknowledge your unwanted self, then your sense of incongruence is decreased and you are back in control. But there is a cost: ignoring your unwanted self limits your self-awareness—and keeps you stuck in the external fight.

- If you surrender to your unwanted self, you decrease your sense of incongruence. But there's also a cost to this option: you hopelessly agree that you are who you don't want to be, and you give up the struggle. You have allowed the conflict with the other to reinforce a limiting view of yourself.

- If, in a proactive stance, you face the unwanted self and at the same time reach for the wanted self, you will be painfully aware of the incongruence but moving toward ultimately increased congruence.

Incongruence can be leveraged for greater peace—both within and with the other. The external trigger from the other creates the opportunity to use the incongruence between *who you are* and *who you want to be* for personal growth—which then also enhances relationship. Yet, as always, the push to change and the pull to stay the same are equally substantial.

So, What Now?

Conflict with the other highlights the incongruence between *who you are* and *who you need to be for the other*. Try the following:

- Refuse to ignore any inner disturbance about who you are—in your role, your community, your family, or any other group—and who you need to be.

- Use that disturbance to ask yourself some important questions: Who do you want to be? What fits and what doesn't? Who do you need to be to feel successful and content—and can you take one action right now to move in that direction?

- Harness your discomfort to create greater alignment inside and out, for long-lasting comfort.

CHAPTER 8

Choosing Change or no Change

In this chapter we'll consider two more opportunities for change. First, we'll address the human propensity to create trouble in relationship and second, we'll explore the "approval ache."

Creating Trouble Is Natural

In Chapter 5 we examined the unwanted self. Although this part of us would like to stay out of trouble, it inadvertently creates a fair bit. How does it do so? Let's contemplate the various ways the unwanted self creates trouble in relationships, so we can begin to do what often feels counterintuitive: solve trouble.

How trouble grows. Do you unconsciously cultivate trouble in your relationships by being less than you are? For instance, if you're a conflict avoider, you might back down in the middle of a family crisis though your valuable input could move the conversation in a constructive direction. Or you might be bamboozled by the other's tactics, even though you are normally insightful and *could* see the tactics for what they are and render them powerless. You have a choice: succumb once more to self-doubt—and other internal barriers—or wrestle through.

Suppose you try to assert yourself and the other accuses you of being selfish, when the truth is that your default position is to be generous. Maybe this time you truly confront the selfish versus unselfish debate in your own head. You may be susceptible to the accusation because it fits with your beliefs about who you think you should be (unselfish) or should not be but fear you really are (selfish, like your mother, who was too self-absorbed). Perhaps you cave in, too, because asserting yourself seems too difficult, and you would rather protect yourself from any potential backlash from the other. Maybe you chronically step away from your fear rather than harnessing it.

By being less than you are, you end up being what you don't want to be. You end up being taken advantage of, overlooked, or dismissed, and the trouble between you and the other continues.

Alternatively, when you step up to be all you want to be, you also invite the best from the other.

Doubling trouble. Often how you respond to unmet needs—feeling rejected, neglected, or not respected—doubles the trouble. Suppose that when you feel rejected you become smothering or relentless in your pursuit of attention; when you feel neglected you pout; or when you feel disrespected you become demanding. Each of these responses—your M.O.—inadvertently aggravates the need, because the behavior pushes the other away rather than draws them close. The other is likely reacting not to your need but to what you do when you feel it. Rather than responding in a way that doubles your initial trouble, see if you can behave well, precisely when your need is unmet.

Tripling trouble. Your behavior in troubling times often makes you feel worse about yourself because you exacerbate the pain of the initial trouble. For example, you might feel pathetic because you so desperately and shamelessly pursued the other. Or you may feel guilty for the damaging words you said in your angry outburst. If you can, learn from the past by remembering how you felt when you acted out, and refuse to repeat the pattern.

For trouble's sake. Do you get caught up in trouble just because you can? You know the habits of your unwanted self. It's difficult to stop troubling behavior when others put up with it *and* it's effective. You control, and the other falls into line. You become chronically helpless, and the other comes to your aid. You complain, yell, give the silent treatment, or spin out of emotional control because you can, and you get results. After a while, you are lulled into thinking your troubling behavior is okay, and the status quo is maintained.

Unfortunately, it's often only when the other no longer tolerates the antics that they're arrested. If you resonate with any of these troubling behaviors, another option is to care for yourself like you would for a needy toddler who is frustrated—soothing yourself so you can make changes unilaterally, even if the other doesn't demand them from you.

As you explore your relationship to trouble, perhaps you will look for a new road that leads to less trouble. This will require you to act differently than you usually do—which we'll cover in Part 5. Suffice it to say, for now, observe your behavior, try doing the opposite, and watch for the results.

Our Ache for Approval Cuts Both Ways

Our inbuilt need for approval harbors many opportunities for change. Will we ever be rid of our need for approval? Maturing reduces it, but doesn't eradicate it entirely. Our need for approval links to our sense of *who we think we need to be*. Our ache for approval is another arena in which we can wrestle through the incongruence between our unwanted and wanted selves and our persona. The approval ache can urge us to grow, or to reinforce the unwanted self. It cuts both ways.

How much should we care about what people think? When we seek an answer to this question by navigating between the polarized positions of caring too much and not caring at all, we enact a necessary internal struggle. But if we choose one position over the other, we snuff out the struggle— the necessary tension that could produce change is lost. The reaching for approval casts light on our potential self. The other person plays a significant role in this unfolding. Staying receptive to the other's approval, or lack of it, leaves us vulnerable, at their mercy. However, because our identity is shaped within contexts, we need this dynamic with the other to help us develop our sense of self.

We are who we are in relation to others. In addition, the other tests the accuracy of our self-image, for instance, when we think we're funny and the other thinks we're rude. Our opinions must be tested against others' opinions, because with brains that protect us to a fault, we can easily delude ourselves (see "The Power of Delusion" in Chapter 12). What the other thinks matters because it helps inform *who we think we need to be*. Fostering openness to feedback promotes change. Because we don't want to be socially isolated and need to belong, our ache for approval provides the necessary push to deal with the unwanted self, bringing our undesirable behavior into line.

Yet to remain fixated on achieving approval from the other is also problematic. Reflect on three natural responses when your needs for approval are unmet:

- You become addicted to your need and move from person to person hoping to get your fix, neglecting to deal with the dependency that makes you vulnerable. Unless you address the critical issue of how much *you* approve of *yourself*, the approval ache refuses to be satiated. The more you get from others, the more you need, and the more dependent you become.

- You keep trying for the approval and, unfortunately, the more you press for it, the less likely you'll get it. People can sense when a desire is just too strong or desperate; they can't give you what you need, because your neediness itself feels unhealthy.

- You limit contact with the person who refuses to fill your need. This action seduces you with the promise of peace, but often, the source of aggravation is difficult to remove because that person is intricately connected to your network. Hence the restlessness is suppressed but remains.

Obviously, the other is not just anybody. Who's approval matters to you? Some people you don't think about at all because they don't trigger you; with others, their approval is a non-issue because you know you have it. Then there are those who really get to you because though you want their approval, it's just beyond your reach, despite your best efforts to win it. This unsettling relationship that consumes your psyche and robs you of peace also holds gems, which is why you can't let it go. Maybe not getting the approval brings into focus something you have not wanted, or been able, to see. When you fail to gain approval from the other, the judgment you feel from them activates your self-judgment and you tell yourself, "I'm too sloppy," or "I'm not smart enough," or "I should be more sensitive," and so on. Or maybe failing to get approval from the significant other causes you to pull away from the dependency and discover dormant strengths waiting to be released and utilized.

The approval ache can be used for change or no change. It can be useful or harmful, as the following scenarios show:

- If getting the approval inoculates you to change and inadvertently encourages you to stay in a self-limiting place, then it is harmful.

- If your need for approval causes you to lose your ability to discern others' expectations of you, then it is harmful. (Their expectations may have everything to do with them and not be relevant to you. Subscribing to their lack of approval can only result in self-defeat.)

- If your need for approval pushes you to be someone you're not, then your stress will only increase, and your need will rob you of being your true self.

- If the approval ache is a compelling incentive that helps you overcome inertia and change, moving you toward who you want to be, it is useful.

- If not getting the approval you crave directs you back to self and enables you to give yourself approval like never before, then it is useful.

- If getting the approval frees you up to no longer be dependent on it and encourages you to be all that you are, then it is a wonderful gift.

So, there you have it. Trouble and approval offer two more opportunities for change—reach for it when you want it. And we don't always want it—or need it! Sometimes change is too much and what we need is to have a nonsensical conversation with life-giving laughter—the kind that suspends all cares and ushers in a new perspective. The next section is about sweet affection for the unwanted self, because before we can deal with it, we need to lovingly hold our unwanted self, compassionately understand it, and warmly embrace it.

So, What Now?

The self you don't want to be can be found in your natural bent to create trouble and in your ache for approval from that someone reluctant to grant it. What would it take for you to choose growth and change, rather than defeat and more of the same? Try the following:

- Describe how you create trouble in your relationships, even give your troublesome habit a name. If you're stuck, ask your friends for help.

- Change your relationships by being your fuller, wanted self, even when it causes you discomfort: behave well when you don't get your needs met, and refuse to misbehave, even when others brook your trouble-making behaviors.

- Consider whose approval you are trying to get. How do you want them to see you?

- Use your ache for approval to help inform who you need and want to be, so that you can approve of yourself more.

CHAPTER 9

Warming Up to the Unwanted Self

We don't normally think about a part of ourselves as "unwanted." We may simply be aware of our inner discomfort while in interaction with the other. The unwanted self has been neglected for too long, needs attention, and only as we befriend it do we come to understand it. That's when we can't help but warm up to it. Let's look more closely at the nature of the unwanted self and why self-limiting beliefs are so powerful. Understanding where it comes from, why it begs to be heard, and the important role it fills helps us validate the unwanted self.

Stuck in a Bind

Who we are and *don't want to be* begs to be dealt with, and who we want to be and *aren't yet* beckons us. As discussed in Chapter 5, the unwanted self is experienced from opposite angles. As a by-product of painful past experiences, the unwanted self is a compelling force to be reckoned with—yet we have no desire to go back to that painful place. And in a strange way, we also hold on to the unwanted self to protect us from more pain or to help us get our needs met. Here's the dilemma: we don't want to be our unwanted self, but we also can't afford to give it up. The following examples illustrate how this might play out:

- "I see that I'm being a bitch. I don't want to be a bitch (it's not who I am or want to be) but I can't tolerate being disrespected."

- "I'm the loud, abrasive, and gruff guy that I don't want to be, but it's the only way I know to protect myself from the pain of not fitting in. 'Suck it up' was drilled into me as a child."

- "I don't want to be the magnet that draws trouble to myself because then I'm the problem. But I also can't tolerate this inequality. My mother repeatedly chooses my sister over me."

- "I want to be kind and compassionate, yet demeaning comments slip out of my mouth. When I don't get what I want, I just become hurtful."

- "I want to be a passionate lover but that makes me feel guilty and self-indulgent. Not being able to let go makes me feel like an inadequate lover."

If we look with empathy, we can't help but warm up to the unwanted self, because it's in such a bind. The unwanted self is simply trying to manage matters in the best way it knows how, making hardy attempts to fend off more pain. Yet here is the problem: running from the pain only entrenches it and further ingrains a self-limiting belief system.

Self-Limiting Beliefs Support the Unwanted Self

The self-limiting beliefs of the unwanted self are difficult to extinguish for any of the following reasons:

- They hold an element of truth that will not be denied. We can point to situations where we were the very thing we don't want to be. Dismissing data is difficult.

- They come with a payoff, at least some of the time. For instance, when I say that I am a loser, another person reassures me with, "It isn't so."

- They feel or were once logical. Adopting the belief "I'm bad" or "It's my fault" reduced trouble in the context in which the belief formed.

- In a backward way, they help us reach for the wanted self. We hold the negative message close so that the pain of it will drive us to achieve. For instance, striving to excel might be driven by another's hurtful comment in the past, such as "You're stupid" because you needed learning assistance. Even though you are immensely successful in your role at work, evidence of smart behavior doesn't necessarily result in a changed view of self. Since incongruence remains, so does the risk of reverting to not striving. You *look* competent but don't necessarily *feel* competent.

- They are such an integral part of our sense of identity that we don't know how to extricate ourselves from them. For instance, your self-limiting belief might be, "I can't stand up for myself," or "I have a weak character." Saying something different to yourself about who you are might only increase your internal conflict.

- Because they are so entrenched, working our way out of self-limiting beliefs seems too difficult for today. Facing our fear and self-doubt will need to wait for another time. It's easy to procrastinate when such self-examination seems especially onerous.

Though our self-limiting beliefs often get a bad rap, when we pull them apart to see how they work, they become understandable. At the same time, they are also damaging because they hold the unwanted self in place and stand in the way of possible transformation. The unwanted self also gets a bad rap, but a closer look lets us hold it affectionately.

Validating Our Unwanted Part

I remember the poignant words I heard when I asked a client to visit her unwanted self: "Why would I go back to that place? I'm afraid I'll be there forever. It's the worst place I know. I don't want to give it power." The unwanted self's "place" might be one of loneliness, despair, or exclusion. The process of becoming more intimate with our unwanted self is somewhat counterintuitive. So perhaps the best way to "go there" is first by trying to understand where and when our unwanted self emerged.

Where did it come from? When we understand the source of our unwanted self, it's easier to compassionately and tenderly embrace ourselves for who we are now. Seeing our unwanted self is like looking back at ourselves as a vulnerable child, doing the best it can, trying to cope and find its way. We wrap our arms around that smaller version of ourselves. What happened back there? What are your first memories of being the person you didn't want to be? Can you tell that story—one that is real, loving, and life-giving while it is stripped of all illusion (even if that creates more anxiety in the short term)?

Why it begs to be heard. The unwanted self has something to say and begs to be heard because in the context in which it developed, the words made sense. Perhaps the unwanted self is a fundamental, highly resilient perception that took root a long time ago, for example, "I'm not enough," "I don't belong," or "I'm too much." The way you experience life reinforces this perception, and perhaps how you currently conduct your life results in the same con- clusion. For instance, maybe you feel inadequate because you don't perform well at work. That may be because you don't apply yourself, or perhaps you strive to be or do something beyond your capability. Or maybe the modus operandi you adopt when your needs aren't met, or when fears run rampant, further feeds the unwanted self. For example, I'm afraid I won't be seen, so I monopolize the conversational space with my personal interests, oblivious to the other until I get home and, upon reflection, feel wretched about my self-absorption.

Just as hearing what the unwanted self has to say can validate it, so can finding a desirable kernel inside it.

Finding the desirable within the undesirable. Even when the unwanted self contains an understandable limitation, within the undesirable is an energy that has value. For instance, I don't like who I become in my anger—either stewing on it or spilling it over those around me. Both are destructive. Yet, unless it's a learned response of frustration, somewhere in the heart of anger is a sense of injustice. The energy source within anger is useful for pushing past barriers, realizing potential, and pursuing that which is right and good. Take laziness as another example. On the undesirable side, laziness might be a cover for something else. If I don't believe that I have the capacity to perform, laziness protects me while it prevents me from getting what I want. Although continually succumbing to slothfulness is obviously self-defeating, being obsessively super-charged also has its problems. What propels a person's need to constantly be "doing?" What looks like laziness to some might be the ability to devote valuable time to life's subtle pleasures that others miss. Looking for the asset inside each liability is not simply Pollyannaism; rather it aims to see a bigger and more complete picture.

The Important Role of the Unwanted Self

As much as we don't like the unwanted self, it grabs our attention and the attention of the other because of its disturbing nature. In that way, the unwanted self directs us to important matters. Here are some of the ways it functions:

- *It alerts us to the other's unacceptable behavior.* I want to be a compassionate and caring daughter yet find myself being miserable and nasty at times. How does this happen? *Not being what I want to be* is worth paying attention to because it informs me of what must happen next. In this scenario, I am likely responding to my mother acting in a way that is not okay. Maybe she's intrusive, critical, overly dependent, or a complainer. She might even be competing with me because I'm doing better than she did. (She's fighting with her own sense of inadequacy.) My bad behavior alerts me to the need to deal with my mother's bad behavior differently than I have until now, because otherwise the unhelpful pattern will remain: feeling bad for being impatient and nasty, and then compensating by capitulating or pacifying when I shouldn't.

- *It points to the limitation that prevents us from dealing with the other's behavior.* Maybe I don't believe I can assert myself because of some self-perceived deficiency. For example, I might think I don't have control of my own emotions. I might fear that I am as neurotic as my mother.

- *It invites outside, potentially transformative pressure.* If the other will not abide endlessly with our unwanted self, a necessary pressure that is potentially transformative builds. Change can come from either side. My mother can refuse to talk to me when I am less than caring, or I can overcome my limitation, learn to assert myself with finesse, and create the potential for each of us to transform.

Let's consider Marney's story as an illustration of a role filled by the unwanted self.

Marney: The Voiceless Bystander

Marney wanted to overturn the pain that she experienced in her family of origin by doing things differently in her own. She wanted to ensure that her children would *not* be embarrassed by her like she was by her parents: a mother who was often absent due to mental instability and an alcoholic father whose emotions were out of control. It made sense that she emerged from such an environment feeling inadequate and with a need to prove that she was different.

With that sense of inadequacy haunting her, she was fearful to speak up in groups and take her rightful space. In light of all the good decisions she had made in her adult life, how was it that the feeling of inadequacy remained? As much as Marney didn't like the constraining belief, over time she came to realize that it served a purpose. It propelled her to create a different life and break from her origins. She was afraid of what would happen if she were to let go of the belief—and she also feared taking the action necessary to eradicate it.

Yet Marney was tired of being a bystander without a voice. She decided that it was time to overcome her fear and speak up. Marney knew the risk: in the aftermath she would feel either more or less adequate. So, she determined that she needed to define success differently. Rather than having to be well-spoken with something clever to say, she simply had to vocalize instead of remaining speechless at important junctures. Otherwise she would never stop feeling inadequate.

An incident at Marney's reading group presented the perfect opportunity. When Olivia carried on in her usual strident treble, Marney responded, "I don't agree …" A debate ensued and the atmosphere became increasingly tense. Marney said to Olivia, "I find your manner somewhat off-putting." Olivia wasn't used to being challenged like this. The looks and snickers around the room left Olivia wondering if others were having difficulty with her as well. Marney's discomfort was palpable—she didn't want to risk Olivia's disapproval. Nothing ended perfectly that evening but there were several rewarding surprises. Two women approached Marney later to tell her their own struggles with speaking freely in the group. The upheaval created some shifts within and between group members. Marney still felt somewhat unsettled when she left, but she also went home feeling more hopeful, freer, and even a little excited.

As Marney's story shows, the unwanted self unbalances us, but as a benefit also connects us to others (as with the two women). When we don't face the unwanted self, it often pushes others away (as with Olivia alienating people in the group) or doesn't pull others close because we're acting as less than we are (for example, Marney did have things to say, but had remained silent in her reading group for a long time). When we face the unwanted self, we feel vulnerable and that potentially connects us to others. When we need each other, intimacy and trust are potentially increased. The unwanted self has something valuable to fight for, but unfortunately it mostly sabotages itself. As we hold the unwanted self affectionately, opportunities for transformation are created.

So, What Now?

Warm up to your unwanted self, because it is a by-product of painful past experiences and functions to protect you from more pain (albeit mostly unsuccessfully). Recognize its important role in the process of change. Try the following:

- Catch yourself in one self-limiting belief per day, challenge it, and substitute it with a believable statement that feeds your wanted self. (Keeping a log can be helpful.)

- Can you see what important role your unwanted self might fill—what is its function? What might it be fighting for?

- Name an earlier painful experience related to your unwanted self and about which you still feel vulnerable. Extend compassion to yourself right now—wrap your arms around a smaller version of you—or ask someone for a hug.

CHAPTER 10

Validating the Internal Struggle

The energy for engaging the fight with the other is found in the collision between our current experience and our internal world. Do we, or do we not, engage the internal struggle? Let's explore three examples that illustrate situations in which external and internal worlds collide.

Benita has a run in with her brother because he challenges the wisdom of a decision she made that will impact the rest of the family. Benita retorts with a comment about his pathetic passivity. "At least someone is taking action," she says. But on the inside Benita feels far less valiant. She is in her old sore spot, feeling like everything is her fault. This thought quickly morphs into "I'm bad"—the person Benita doesn't want to be.

Deseado hopes for some action with his wife, Tonia, tonight. He has attended to the children and dutifully checked off chores from the list. He initiates with several romantic gestures but receives little response from Tonia. Feeling rejected (once again), Deseado's vulnerability increases. He becomes the needy puppy dog, saying to her, "You don't love me," which is not wildly attractive to Tonia. Deseado would feel so much better if only she would take the edge off his sense of insecurity by reassuring him that he is indeed desirable and lovable. He is left to struggle with who he thinks he is, precisely when the reassurance he craves is not forthcoming.

The boss says to Karel, "I've heard some rumblings from people in your unit about you being a micromanager." Karel responds with some choice words about the unreliability of several employees who are making his life difficult. He stands up for himself with, "I'm just ensuring that you get what you need." Karel must decide what to do with the feedback. He could write off his "irresponsible staff," or he could look more closely to see if his behavior is contributing to the complaints. How quickly does he take control, and how much control does he need to have? What is the impact of his need for control on the employees that report to him? Karel has a choice: to sit with the discomfort and address his controlling nature, or to defend it.

Conflict with the other activates our internal identity struggle between what we think of ourselves and who we really are. Our sense of identity drives the conflict. We might fight the perception the other has of us. Maybe we don't agree and try to change the other's mind. Or maybe inwardly we agree but don't want it to be so. Sometimes we make a negative inference about our identity before the other does. For instance, "The other didn't say I was an idiot, but that is what I think they were *really* saying." The other may or may not have been saying this about you, but that's secondary to a more fundamental issue: the other has activated a vulnerable and restless part of your identity where you question yourself.

If we choose not to engage the struggle within, then we step further away from the self and begin to de-individuate, which means that our ability to self-evaluate is decreased—yet that ability is critical. Without it, we can easily destroy the other and the relationship, and when that happens, a part of us is usually also decimated. Choosing not to engage the internal struggle leaves us susceptible to the vicious cycle of defending, blaming, and protecting—a cycle that begins to spin faster and more frequently. Though we could use the struggle to end the useless fighting, reinforcing the unwanted self is unfortunately often a compelling temptation.

Two Ways We Reinforce the Unwanted Self
Significant "change moments" hold two distinct possibilities: either we act to reinforce the unwanted self, or we feed the wanted self. When we turn on ourselves in defeat, we reinforce the unwanted self, and depending on what we do with shame, it can be useful and feed the wanted self, or it can be debilitating and reinforce the unwanted self.

Turning on ourselves. We don't always take the internal fight outward; instead we sometimes go inward and turn on ourselves. We accept a put-down as being the truth about who we are, which reinforces the unwanted self. We might think fighting against the negative message is too complicated, too much work, and will bring with it only more internal disturbance. By caving in to the negative messages (for example, that I'm a failure, a loser, or unworthy) we make the incongruence in our own heads disappear.

Shame: useful or debilitating? Shame sounds like a pejorative term because of our experience of it, but what happens if we shield ourselves from shame entirely? Is there a legitimate place for appropriate and useful shame? Certain of our behaviors invite shame because they betray who we want to be. Sometimes the pressures we feel from others or the situation help us make the change we desire. For example, I'm ducking in and out of traffic and then look over and notice that the person I just cut off is someone I know—someone who's opinion of me matters—and I'm already feeling her disapproval. "Busted," I think. "I *am* only thinking about myself." I am mortified and can't bring myself to even look over into the other car. I have humiliated myself by my own behavior and need to make a change. Shame is appropriate and most useful when it helps feed the *wanted* self.

Lamentably, giving in to debilitating shame is easy. Surrendering in self-defeat is costly because we agree that we cannot be who we think we need to be, or that we are who the other says we are (when that's not who we *want* to be). In such a case, *we have given up the necessary internal fight.* The conflict then keeps us on a negative inner track that reinforces the unwanted self as an inescapable reality, eroding a healthy sense of self. If there is a perceived power difference between us and the other, the damage will be direr.

Another notable aspect of shame is that it grows in secrecy. Without exposure, our shameful story of abuse, deception, repeated failure, or guilty pleasure remains unchallenged. That story needs to be revisited with a new experience of self so that it can be overturned. Perhaps we adopt a new perspective and the past no longer holds the same sting, for example, instead of feeling shame for being the child from the wrong side of the tracks, I begin to see myself as a resilient, courageous person who overcame immense odds. Or perhaps I succumbed to the shame of some guilty pleasure, but a new situation gives me the opportunity to align my current behaviors with my values, thereby returning to, or stretching toward, the self I want to be.

Choosing to Feed the Wanted Self

In the most trying moments, either we step up to the challenge and feed the wanted self or we step down in defeat and reinforce the unwanted self.

A puck gets past the goalie and slips into the net. What the goalie thinks next will affect the future of the game more than the goal just scored. What does the goalie believe about who she is while the puck is in the net? Self-beliefs are core at this juncture. The booing of the fans may make it easier for the goalie to succumb to the self-defeating beliefs of the unwanted self (for example, that she's not capable). If the goalkeeper quits, then the sensation of incongruence between the wanted (competent) and unwanted (incompetent) selves disappears.

However, the other option for the goalie is to use this critical moment to feed the wanted self. In addressing her self-doubt, the internal disturbance will momentarily increase. The push from the external expectations of fans, team, and family, along with her own notions of who she needs to be at this moment, could work together to *feed* her wanted self: by working through her self-doubt, she strengthens the wanted self, and now has the words with which to overcome the negative voice. "I can do it. I've got what it takes to pull through when things are not looking good."

Since self-doubt is such a significant part of the internal struggle, let's explore it further.

Self-Doubt Reinforces the Unwanted Self

Self-doubt is a natural by-product of the system at work. It's what trips us up and makes us susceptible to resuming old patterns, particularly when the other challenges us.

Encountering pushback. The other's resistance to what you have to say feeds your self-doubt. Some resistance is so subtle that you wouldn't even label it as such at the outset. For instance, you might present your opinion with conviction and fervor, explaining how the current state is intolerable and you need change. The other responds by being empathetic, patient and understanding. Though this doesn't feel like resistance, it functions as such. Faced with this response, you de-escalate and your position softens. The other has effectively disarmed you and you have lost your certainty.

Another kind of pushback might not be so subtle. You have finally made a decision and then the other has a barrage of questions, which leaves you floundering. You couldn't possibly have considered all angles, nor can you substantiate every opinion with data. For instance, perhaps you and your partner are accustomed to making many significant decisions in tandem. This might sound like a good thing, but it also has its downsides. Since the two of you are stalemated on an issue, you decide to go ahead on your own instead of reaching consensus first. Your partner pushes back by stepping out of the decision-making process entirely. You are left alone to bear the responsibility for the potential ramifications of your action, which frightens you. It's too much, too fast.

Whether the pushback is subtle or blatant, it's effective and it's custom-tailored for you. The other knows your weakness and consciously or unconsciously plays right to it. That's what we do when we are feeling threatened by the possibility of change.

Certainty gives way to doubt. At what point does your certainty give way to self-doubt? See if any of the statements listed below resonate with you:

- "Maybe I do expect too much."

- "Maybe I can't be satisfied."

- "Maybe I'm not emotional enough."

- "Maybe I'm too emotional."

- "Maybe I'm too difficult."

As the other pokes in and around our weakest area, our clarity dims, uncertainty emerges, and confusion sets in. The other sounds so convincing, their defense so logical and their questions so penetrating. Our confidence erodes and we begin to seriously question ourselves. We might ask, "What if it's a big mistake?" or "What if ... this happens, or that happens ... What then?" The energy required for action has effectively been snuffed out, and we succumb to self-doubt.

Working with fear to wrestle through self-doubt. We might be fearful of the possible ramifications of moving forward despite the outside pressure from the other. If we freely and fully speak our mind, what will the consequences be? If we act, will we have to pay in some form? Will we be able to live with the possible fallout? Staying within the constraints of the fence is tempting.

Here we make a critical choice: either we cave in to fear, or we wrestle through. If we surrender to our fear, then we will need to abandon the concern that made us confront the other in the first place, otherwise we will be dizzy with the cognitive dissonance reverberating in our brain. Hence, we might downplay or dismiss our concerns with thoughts such as, "It was silly," "I need to think more about the other," or "I made too big a deal of it." In turning down the volume on our own voice and increasing the volume of the other's, we sidestep our fears (at least temporarily) and calm sets in. We have given up the challenge and reverted to old patterns. The dustup was for naught.

Even though we have surrendered to the fear, there is likely a niggling voice that doesn't quite let us go. We aren't convinced that the path we chose is sustainable. We suspect that this issue is not really gone and that it will resurface. We are disappointed in ourselves for caving in. We have also lost some self-respect, because we see ourselves doing the same thing we did in the past, even though it frustrated us then. For a fleeting moment, we might even wonder if giving in this time will cause us to do something even more radical and hurtful in the future. But we run from that thought too.

If we face fear rather than succumb to fear, we venture onto a more difficult road, but a road with more options. We dismissed our own voice because of fear. When we face fear, we once again invite our voice back in (and anxiety increases). Fear signals that it's time to move. It's a natural emotion that accompanies the need for change. Changing is not acting *from* the fear or *because* of the fear, but rather working *with* the fear; harnessing fear's energy to propel us forward. If the fear still seems too overwhelming, then an intermediary step is required. You may need to stay where you are to build up sufficient strength and resources to successfully engage the next opportunity that presents itself.

Working through self-doubt entails transcending unnecessary barriers and overcoming false limitations. Courageously, you forge into uncharted territory and build confidence by engaging in action that boosts your competency levels. What action do you need to take? Do you need to do a little more research, spend more time on preparation, talk to the right people, increase your knowledge base with a class, or get your credentials? What have you thought you were not capable of before but realize that you are now? Can you stretch beyond your comfort zone to increase your capacity for risk? Can you increase your tolerance for failure? (What would you rather do: be paralyzed, sometimes for years, because you're not sure of the right decision, or act and find a way to live with imperfection?) Addressing and overcoming your self-doubt creates the opportunity for a new dance. Perhaps this time you conclude that you can't afford to back off.

Self-doubt reinforces the unwanted self, keeping us in a no-change position. Hence facing that which holds us back is fundamental. Self-doubt then becomes the edge where we push through our fears, the place where we don't quite trust ourselves, and where our confidence is flagging. If we refuse to cave in to self-doubt, then we'll realize that we're capable of more than we knew. That's the upside of self-doubt.

An encouraging postscript: the initial working through of barriers in self-doubt takes considerable effort, but the success in doing so is surprisingly transferrable—it makes future barriers easier to overcome. For instance, gaining victory in one area of self-discipline, such as weight management, can improve your skills in other areas, such as managing finances or time.

The next section acknowledges the difficulty in embracing self and at the same time highlights the consequences of *not* embracing self. Let's now explore this important aspect of the internal struggle.

Six Reasons to Embrace Self

Failure to embrace self is costly: we project that self on to others, we do stupid things, and we are still at risk and stuck. Embracing self, on the other hand, comes with benefits: we find it easier to embrace the other and we become our most compelling self. Let's consider the six reasons in turn.

If we don't embrace self, we project that self on to others. Projection is at the root of much interpersonal conflict. Humans don't like it when another is their mirror, yet seeing ourselves in the other, is how healing often occurs. Projection works on the homeopathic principle of "like cures like." We are unconsciously attracted to a person who manifests the very characteristic that we ourselves are struggling with but haven't owned yet. For instance, I might talk incessantly about my mother-in-law's controlling nature but can't see my own. I might be upset by the aggressive nature of a colleague while neglecting my own assertiveness. I could be perturbed that my colleague never works overtime, but the truth is that my own life is out of balance and I don't play enough. These reflections mirrored in the other are disturbing because they activate the part we have repressed.

That which we neglect becomes part of our dark shadow self and inhabits the unconscious mind. Hence, we don't recognize that when we fight the other, we are actually fighting ourselves. Or we may neglect a positive part of us that then morphs into an unwanted self because it doesn't find expression—when we have substantial wisdom but don't yet see it nor find the courage to speak it, for example.

If we don't embrace self, we are still at risk. We might have the inner fortitude to white-knuckle it and manifest good behavior for years. But most people experience some significant situation wherein their "best foot forward" slips back. Newspapers are full of stories about a model citizen (by all appearances) caught doing something heinous. Or we find out that a family member or friend is guilty of some transgression and we think, "I can't believe it. I would never have imagined that of them." We can look even closer to home. During an escalating conflict, I might surprise myself by erupting with lethal, ugly rage that spews out at the other. My thoughts are so violent that they scare me and I think, "Where did this come from?" Perhaps that capacity for rage was always there and feels foreign only because, until now, no situation had caused it to explode.

If we don't embrace self, we do stupid things. Insecurity has many faces and makes us act strangely. The enemy is not outside; rather it is inside us. An overabundance of attention-grabbing actions—that personally we don't see—becomes nauseating to others. Making insulting comments or ignoring the other when we long for acceptance are actions puzzling to the other. Our unnecessarily taking things personally becomes taxing for those around us. Making outlandish statements for attention becomes old. Trying too hard when we long to be appreciated becomes wearisome for everyone involved, and pretending we are someone we are not eventually breaks down.

In many cases, who we are is not really the problem—rather, our behaviors are the problem, because they prevent us from getting what we want.

We work against ourselves when we have no intention of doing so. We push a person away when we want them close. When we like someone too much, we might walk right past them because we don't want to botch it. When fear takes hold, behavior often becomes nonsensical. Embracing self does not mean that insecurity automatically vanishes; rather, it means befriending insecurity instead of running from it.

If we don't embrace self, we are still stuck. When we fail to embrace ourselves, we continue protecting and defending, and the old fights just keep cycling. Or maybe we have stopped reacting and are simply despairing. Maybe we have capitulated to a view of self that's painful: "I'm a fake," "I can't get it right," or "The other will never be satisfied with me." Embracing self is about facing the truth of what we are and stepping up to be who we want to be. That might mean acceptance and change or it might simply mean acceptance.

Embracing self makes it easier to embrace the other. When a spirit of judgment is no longer turned inward, it's easier to give up the outward judgment of the other. In embracing ourselves, we have created space to see the other more clearly. We see reality for what it is rather than viewing the faults of the other disproportionately. Previously, our vision was clouded by our unresolved issues. By embracing ourselves, we also have increased energy because we're no longer fighting inside, and this enables us to focus on the other.

Embracing self produces the most compelling and infectious me. Embracing our full self, the unsavory along with the savory, ultimately produces the most compelling and infectious me. When we are less than whole we are like a stick figure: one-dimensional, lifeless, and sterile. Our wholeness forms in the struggle between our opposing natures. We are kind and we are mean. We are truthful and we lie. We are generous and we are tight-fisted. We are gracious and we withhold. We are accepting and we are hopelessly judgmental. To grapple with the contradictions within is to be human, and this creates the depth and breadth that makes us soulful in encounters with others.

This chapter has validated the internal struggle and presented us with a worthy challenge: Will we refuse to reinforce the unwanted self and instead choose to feed the wanted self? Making that choice involves letting ourselves feel what we don't want to feel as we confront our shame, fears, self-doubt, and shadow selves. Change requires a hot cognition, in which heart and head are engaged. That's when following up with action has the best chance of success.

So, What Now?

Respect the difficulty of engaging the internal struggle and applaud yourself for small victories. After warming up to the unwanted self, refuse to reinforce it and choose instead to feed the wanted self so that you can embrace a fuller you. Consider the following:

- Are you aware of a debilitating shame within? What could you do to refuse that indictment so you don't feel defeated? What useful shame do you need to accept so that it propels you to line up with the self you want to be?

- Since self-doubt is both your weakest link and a pivotal point for change, address one of your self-doubts and wrestle through the fear that the other activates.

- When that someone really gets to you, ask yourself if you are projecting on to them an unwanted part of yourself. As with homeopathy, like cures like. So use what you discover about yourself to cure rather than feed the conflict between you.

- Reflect on several significant relationships. When you fail to embrace yourself, how do you behave and what is the cost to your relationship? When you embrace a fuller you, what benefits do you experience?

- Reflect on a relationship in which you feel most comfortable bringing your full self and rest in the warmth of that.

CHAPTER 11

Doing It: Engaging with the Fight Within

This chapter presents possible steps to engage the fight within. Though the steps are presented sequentially here, in real time there is usually a gap between facing the unwanted self and embracing the self. Different steps are required at the various stages in your journey. Pick the strategies that currently fit and, as always, feel free to create your own.

Finding the Way Out by Making Connections Within

Going deeper in requires making connections among internal "happenings" which are not immediately evident. One purpose of going deeper in is to claim these happenings and bring them into consciousness. Here is a scenario that demonstrates the difficulty and the importance of making connections within.

Ludmila is upset because she heard some titillating information about her good friend from a third party, who now wants her to keep it a secret. Ludmila wants to reveal all, saying she doesn't believe in secrets because they are harmful. She makes a convincing case, and at one level her reasoning sounds legitimate. But Ludmila fails to acknowledge the real reason for telling all: she wants to avoid the pain of being on the outside. That's the connection Ludmila isn't making. If other people think she knew before, then she might be spared the pain (this occurs mostly unconsciously). Ludmila defaults to her old M.O. of "I must get attention." She doesn't link her reaction to her fears ("I will be excluded") and her self-doubt ("I don't know what's inappropriate"), which feed the very thing she doesn't want to be—inadequate. Unfortunately, by allowing her M.O. to divert her from the pain, Ludmila reinforces her unwanted self, because, once again, she is pushed aside.

The way out of conflict entails seeing the connections among the components of yourself that might not seem related at the outset. Become curious about how these various components relate and collude to maintain the status quo. Together, they work like a well-oiled machine *against* change, rather than *for* it. Beliefs and behavior reinforce the unwanted self, behavior and fears feed self-doubt, beliefs maintain the trigger, and the M.O. unwittingly invites more resistance from the other. Unless …

If you become a little *reflective* rather than *reflexive*, examine the internal system to see how it works, honor it, and then step in a new direction at a significant juncture, you may find your way out of the struggle. That is the hopeful and lonely truth.

Staying with the Sore Spot

To gain ground, stay with the sore spot—even though doing so feels counterintuitive. The natural response is to make one quick, reflexive move away, like when we touch a hot element. We are no more willing to engage with emotional pain than we would purposely endure physical pain. But the sore spot needs a little TLC. The pain cuts deep because it is one of our most tender areas. The gift of our unique contribution to the world often germinates right here, which makes our sore spot highly valuable. Let's discuss how to recognize, acknowledge, and embrace our sensitivities.

Learn to trust the live wire. Healing the sensitivity begins by trusting the live wire that has been triggered. As wretched as a potent negative reaction feels, stick with it, because it has awakened something significant and therefore useful. (You wouldn't have such a strong reaction if that wasn't the case.) Let that strong reaction lead you to the important stuff that's worth fighting for—healing the sensitivity. What is working you up? What stings or makes you the most incensed? Listen to that moment when you say, "I can't believe you said …", because the words that end that sentence lead you to the pain behind the live wire. Among all the things that *were* said, the live wire is the word or phrase that sticks. For instance, in a testy interchange between Lola and Breanna, the words that bit Lola were, "I feel miserable when I talk to you." What hurt Breanna was thinking Lola considered her selfish. They were in conflict because both Lola's and Breanna's view of self was being challenged. Neither saw herself the way she understood the other did, or each wanted to prove the other's perception wasn't valid.

Resist the tempting detours. Taking a detour that leads away from self and around the pain is hugely tempting because the other's problematic behavior provides plenty of fuel. You might respond to a trigger by saying, "I can't believe you said such a stupid and insensitive thing," or "Where do you get off speaking to me like that!" The other's misdeeds and misspoken words give you ample reason to focus on them instead of you. Even though there is likely some validity to how you react to the other, such a response will easily divert you from the more important work of healing your sensitivity—a task that, unfortunately, the other is not in a position to help you with at this point.

Work with the primitive brain. When your spore spot is triggered, pay attention to and work with your primitive brain. The amygdala in the limbic system is doing just what it was designed to do: work heroically to protect you from a perceived threat. The amygdala will not be silenced, particularly if it's not acknowledged. The primitive brain is worth listening to, because it alerts the neocortex to the need to heal your sensitivities. The amygdala doesn't always assess threat correctly, and therefore the neocortex needs to collaborate with the amygdala to determine whether danger is present. If the amygdala is responding to hurts from the past, how much validity is there to the fears in the present? If your neocortex gauges that no current threat exists, then the fear can begin to dissipate. Beliefs that took root at an earlier life stage might lose some of their power when they're revisited; traumatic experiences might be demystified. You are likely in a very different emotional/psychological place than you were when the original fears first took hold.

Sidle up to the sensitivity. In the heat of conflict, we often feel an urgent, compelling need to act on the sensitivity aroused. And well you might ask: "What do I do with the sensitivity?" What if all you need to do is grant yourself time? Try to give yourself time to approach the sensitivity, open to it, make space for it, and accept it, rather than defend against it or pretend it doesn't exist. You might visualize inviting the very part that you've been running from to do nothing but sit with you in an internal room of your own creation. Perhaps you imagine a beautifully sunlit room with a comfy couch and decorated with warm, calming, happy colors. If you can sit with the sensitivity, the pain begins to subside and eventually dissolve as, almost automatically, you begin to integrate the original, unwelcome thought. You might think, "Maybe I am too opinionated and do shut others down prematurely." Maybe, with time, another thought settles in: "I'm glad I have opinions and now I just have to learn to make space for others." In contrast, refusing to sidle up to the sensitivity in the invisible world where the restless identity lives (see the Inner Conflict Map, page 48) makes you vigilant, always expending energy in the visible world, feeding the self-reinforcing loop.

Facing the Unwanted Self

We are stuck with the other because the conflict has taken us to where we're stuck with ourselves. A squirm factor indicates how close we are to that sensitive part that holds us in the fight with others. We conceal it from ourselves, usually because we associate it with a sense of shame. We fight against the unwanted self, using our M.O. to convince the other that they are wrong about us. Facing the unwanted self involves naming the limitation and giving up the counterproductive fight to have the right fight.

First, name the limitation. The stronger you fight against something, the more likely it is that it's a truth worth looking at. Since the unwanted self is what limits you, it begs to be dealt with. It is your catalyst for transformation. What if you could acknowledge, name, and own what you've been fighting against? If you cannot name it, you have not yet identified it. You might ask for help from those around you.

There are endless variations of the unwanted self: you don't want to be selfish, mean, harsh, cold, or stingy, but sometimes you are. Or you want to be self-disciplined, reliable, kind, generous, or considerate, but sometimes you aren't. Maybe something else undoes you. Consider the following possibilities:

- "It's all my fault," which leads you to, "I'm bad."

- "I'm not enough," which begets, "I am unlovable and will always be lonely."

- "I'm incompetent," and therefore, "I am insignificant."

- "I'm not important," and so, "I am not loved."

Or perhaps you really do dislike your own child and fear your rage. Maybe you know that you cause undue hurt to another and you could care less. Perhaps you know you shouldn't be in a particular relationship but can't find the courage within you to leave, even though you're aware you're staying for the wrong reasons. In that case ...

Give up the counterproductive fight and face the truth. Once you've named the limitation, the way out of inner turmoil is to do battle with it—and yourself. Perhaps it is true and you are the very thing you don't want to be. Instead of turning away from this fact or defending yourself, face yourself and let the reflective thoughts, questions, and feelings forge new pathways. It will be tempting to shut down this potentially unsettling process prematurely, when you still feel a modicum of comfort. You've got to find some grit to endure the label and state of mind that you abhor. Flinch and keep witnessing. Let the label do its work on you, taking you to ever-deeper levels of self-awareness. Give up the counterproductive fight to have a productive fight with yourself. Facing yourself takes time.

Embracing Self
When the timing is right for you, move toward embracing self, using any steps that fit for your situation.

Take a transitional step. Initially, approaching the unwanted self can be so distasteful that taking an intermediate step makes acceptance easier. Name what you want to be, affirming that sometimes you are that, and then admitting that sometimes you're not that too. For example, "I am unselfish and I'm selfish," "I'm enough and I'm not enough," "I'm not mean and I am mean." Acknowledging the positive quality before the more negative one is a transitional step.

Hold the two parts of yourself in tension. Holding the positive and negative qualities in tension is more than a transitional step. Until now, you may have been flipping back and forth between them. It's time to pull them together, recognizing we're the sum of our dualities.

Because of our need for simplicity and certainty, adopting a singular identity (projecting that we're just one thing—for example, generous) is more seductive than creating space for a complex identity. Yet the truth is that we are both generous *and* stingy. As the dualities within us duke it out, we recognize that no choice is cheap; decisions made have multiple dimensions. Accepting a complex identity allows the pluses and minuses to influence each other. What happens when our self-negating voice speaks to our self-affirming voice? Which voice speaks to what situation? How will each voice impact the other and our sense of who we are? What would healthy integration of the two voices be?

If we accept our complex identity, does it mean that we simply surrender to the contradictions and anything goes, giving ourselves permission to be one way or the other when doing so suits us? One might say, "This is just who I am," "I'm not going to change—get over it," or "I'm impatient," "I'm blunt," "I'm unkind … Oh well, it's a character flaw!" We can easily convince ourselves that a situation warrants our behavior. Since we are programmed to keep our internal state stable, we don't always risk the upset of reflecting on where we've gone wrong—almost anything can become completely understandable. What if we become so comfortable with our unwanted parts that we don't care about how we hurt the other? Then the other is forced to adopt a self-protective stance.

Alternatively, saying, "I am what I am" might be the acknowledgement of truth—often precipitated by pressure from the outside—and the realization dawns: "Ah, I see it now! I don't keep my promises and trust has broken down," or "I do drink too much—and it's creating relational havoc and the consequences could be severe."

Rather than dismissing one part of ourselves for the other, we let the discrepancies stand to inform and influence each other.

Make a realistic assessment. The conflict trigger highlights a characteristic that you're uncomfortable with. You are left to realistically assess the truth of a duality within. What are you okay with and what are you not okay with? Have you acknowledged the truth to yourself? Even now the temptation to put yourself in the best light possible is compelling.

Suppose you think your unwanted self is "not enough." At first it seems that energy should then be directed to *being enough*, and you think, "Damn it. Everyone should be enough." For some people that position could be healthy. However, what if your pain of not being enough is connected to a conscious or unconscious desire to be superior to someone else? What if you really want to maintain an image because doing so obscures a sense of inferiority that you haven't named, even to yourself?

Or suppose that the self you don't want to be is the person "not listened to." Again, the first thought might be that everyone should be listened to. And perhaps your unique, worthwhile challenge is learning to be heard by exercising capabilities that you haven't yet realized. In another situation, a move toward psychological health might be acknowledging when you should *not* be listened to—for example, if you're filled with anxiety and it spills on to those around you. (Feel free to substitute other characteristics, such as irritability, impatience, or self-absorption.) Which of your concerns should become a concern of the other?

Let's look more closely at how your anxiety might affect the other. If the relationship is important to them and impacts their life, they must take your concern into consideration and at the same time be incredibly discerning about adopting it themselves—a process conducive to self-doubt. The other wonders, "Am I wrong?" or "What if something bad does happen?" If they cave to your excessive anxiety, it's a lose-lose situation—neither of you moves past where you get stuck. However, if the other works through their self-doubt, their confidence is increased, and if you use the other's resistance to reassess your anxiety, you can deal with your issue *and* you get listened to. This is a genuine win-win.

A negative internal voice is too important to dismiss, because it represents work to be done. If you neglect an underlying thought, such as "I'm not competent," "I'm not trustworthy," or "I'm not kind," you risk overlooking a truth that could lead to growth. Focusing on what you think *you are not* allows you to begin to transform into *what you can be.*

Work with acceptance and change. The positives and negatives of your character now sit side by side, where they can influence each other, fight, or become integrated. In this process, acceptance of self is critical. Where you are makes sense in the myriad of your life's experiences. You have simply been coping in the best way you know how. Perhaps now you come to see the unwanted self differently, warm up to it, and are content to integrate it into your sense of self as is. The change could be simply viewing the unwanted self differently, or it might involve embarking on a manageable change program.

Confront Self-Sabotage

Getting unstuck hinges on what you do with the recognition of your unwanted self. It has been said that the greatest distance is between the head and the heart, and to be sure the distance is great. Yet, judging from the difficulty we have in making changes, the distance between the heart and the legs is arguably even further. If only acting were as simple as the Nike slogan, "Just do it." Changing behavior involves a considerable internal struggle, which is why this section explores the problem of self-sabotage.

Often, we work against ourselves with our behavior, thoughts, and feelings, and yet feel helpless to stop doing so. The root word of "sabotage" is the French word *sabot* or "wooden shoe." Such shoes were thrown into textile looms in fifteenth-century Netherlands to break the cogs, as workers were afraid they would be replaced by automated machines. Just like the actions of medieval Dutch weavers, self-sabotaging seems crazy while we are in it, but the behavior makes sense on some level.

Self-sabotage is an outward manifestation of our internal competing parts. We want to be physically fit and yet we want to stay nestled on the couch. The internal fight is on but we are also operating with a few handicaps. We may not even be fully aware of some of our constraining self-beliefs. We haven't yet acknowledged them or can't yet articulate them. We might also have a low tolerance for some emotions—sadness, disappointment, or fear. When an emotion is too upsetting, we adopt a behavior that lessens the miserable feeling, even if a worthy goal is thwarted in the meantime.

Take a simple example. To reduce my state of anxiety, I might reach for a cigarette, even though I want to stay healthy. Giving up any negatively reinforcing behavior, such as smoking, always forces us to increase our tolerance for discomfort, at least in the short term, with a promise of more long-term comfort. This internal fight between our competing parts happens mostly in the unconscious mind, which makes it particularly powerful. Sabotage is obstruction by secret means.

Here is an example of how self-sabotage might work. In this case, the unwanted self is "I can't." If I haven't acknowledged, faced, and dealt with my "I can't" self-belief, then I might construct a fanciful world of "I can," to make myself feel better. In the short term, my illusions of being more than I am may be reinforcing. Yet if the "I can" is not based on fact, eventually I mess up big time (for example, I've convinced everyone, including myself, that I have the skills to run an organization, but at the end of the fiscal year, the budget is woefully unbalanced and the nonprofit is in financial dire straits. I experience a resounding "I can't," and my feeling of being inadequate is agonizingly reinforced.)

Observing the role of the unwanted self in self-sabotaging behavior is fascinating. The unwanted self remains steadfastly in place, with purpose. In the scenario above, the unwanted self ("I can't") shields an even greater pain. If I truly embraced "I can't," I would also have to face another crushing disappointment and grief, such as "I'm less than what I thought I would be," and "My life is less."

What would you have to do to get past self-sabotage? Here are some suggestions:

- Converse with yourself more. Resist the temptation to abandon the conversation prematurely for comfort's sake, and let competing parts hash it out.

- Reflect until you can identify what holds the self-sabotaging pattern in place. What is the greater pain that you don't want to face?

- Tie the self-sabotaging behaviors to their consequences and seriously consider the pros and cons of actions taken and not taken.

- Admit how your self-sabotaging behavior maintains your unwanted self and prevents your realizing goals and the life you imagine.

- Increase your tolerance for difficult emotions. Instead of removing disappointment and loss, find a way to gracefully weave them into your story.

- Confront and assess how realistic your own expectations of yourself are and how realistic others' expectations of you are.

Though self-sabotage is completely understandable, it's also costly. Overcome self-sabotage one incident at a time rather than succumb to a defeatist view of self. Life is long.

Address the Truth

Addressing truth requires a second look at actions taken or not taken—because behavior is evidence that doesn't lie. Many people have made notable attempts to embrace self by adopting positive self-talk. If that's not working, why not? Positive self-talk doesn't eradicate truth. For instance, I can tell myself I am lovable and try to convince the people around me of it and that they should love me, while the truth is that sometimes I really *am* unlovable. I fear that I'm not lovable because deep inside I know that I continually enact unlovely behavior that alienates the other. Truth isn't easily dismissed, and no significant change happens without addressing it.

If we can stay with the truth of the "unwanted self" and do something about it, then we make significant progress, freeing us up to live less defensively. What follows are three examples of how to address the truth. Use these to draft your own action challenges:

- Instead of being judgmental, I will foster curiosity by asking questions that will help me see beyond my limited understanding—something like, "Could you tell me more about how you see the situation from your perspective?"

- I will work on not "being stupid," by committing to learning, to really listening, and to becoming informed.

- When I collapse into passivity, I will refuse to make my customary excuses. Instead I will feel my fear while I take at least one new step.

Relief comes when we stop resisting truth and focus on change. Insight without subsequent action is hollow. Notice that the changes are not big, sweeping changes that will completely alter your life; rather, a change might be one small, manageable step that modifies our direction slightly. After all, even a mammoth tanker eventually changes course, and sometimes it does so with the help of a tiny tugboat.

So, What Now?

Apply strategies that will help you face your unwanted self and embrace yourself more fully. Try the following:

- Tend to your sore spot as you would to a helpless child who has been harmed. Stay with your pain because it gives you an opportunity to heal your sensitivity.

- When naming your unwanted self, trust only the answer that makes you squirm, and use that discomfort to help you change.

- Reach out first for your wanted self and then pull in your unwanted self.

- Instead of succumbing to self-sabotage, face the greater pain that it shields you from.

- Revisit and revise your identity any time you want to leverage conflict for personal success.

PART 4
DISCOVERING THE VALUE
OF THE FIGHT WITHIN

When you apply the inner fight to the challenges and opportunities that inevitable conflict brings, both you and the other realize valuable benefits.

CHAPTER 12

Removing Roadblocks to Seeing Ourselves

Though everyone benefits when we use the external fight to face the internal fight, still, mostly unconsciously, we erect roadblocks: we hold limiting beliefs, we give in to self-delusion, and we become anesthetized by guilt. Over time, we opt for living with extreme inner conflict instead of confronting ourselves and the other. That's a costly detour, because it blocks our journey of growth and our enjoyment of relationship.

Limited Beliefs Unveiled

If you're a lover of art, you know the anticipation of art unveiled. Perhaps you have been following an artist for some time, have caught wind of a new piece in development, and eagerly await the viewing date. You arrive at the gallery and, along with everyone else, wait patiently for the moment when the soft black veil is pulled back, affording a glimpse of that which has been hidden from view. You see the finished product and wonder about the idea that spawned its creation, the influences that shaped it, and the permutations it has undergone since the work began.

Beliefs, too, often exist behind a veil. Life's artistic brush works away and beliefs are birthed and shaped, and they evolve. Our belief system is like a bed we fall into—our place of rest. We lie on something solid and we trust it. Our belief system represents our conclusions about what does and doesn't work, and about what we can expect from ourselves, the other, and the world.

We wrap beliefs around us like a comforting duvet, even when the beliefs are not altogether comforting—but they are what we know. Some beliefs we can articulate, while others exist in a subconscious realm and we become aware of them only when they're elicited by circumstances. One function of conflict is to draw back the veil and reveal the belief that dictates our behavior.

When we engage in the internal conflict that the fight with the other triggers, our certainty is replaced with uncertainty; we must revisit our beliefs, and change has a chance. For example, Jadon's business partner, Ted, says to him, "I don't agree with the way you do sales. You think only about yourself and could care less about the customer." Ouch! This is not who Jadon wants to be and he can feel the disrespect oozing from Ted. He's tempted to defend himself by dismissing Ted's words. Instead, he stays with the rising conflict within and takes a moment to reflect on the beliefs that drive how he does his job. Jadon asks himself, "What do I believe? How is that impacting what Ted thinks of me?" Taking the opportunity of conflict to learn about himself, he uncovers a long-held belief: "If you don't make yourself number one, you will be left behind." In the weeks that follow he comes to realize that acting out his belief has also caused others to reject him—for example, when their biggest client doesn't invite Jadon to play golf with him and Ted—which has, in turn, reinforced the belief.

Conflict with the other provides the opportunity to examine our beliefs, though discerning helpful from hurtful beliefs can be difficult because of the subtleties involved. Holding on to beliefs that keep us in a no-change position is tempting. Yet over time those same beliefs hem us in, limit us, and maintain unnecessary conflict between us and the other. If we don't use the conflict to challenge our beliefs, then it will likely reinforce them. On the other hand, by using inner conflict we can see ourselves for who we really are, take hold of life-giving beliefs, and have more rewarding relationships. The other helps us get there.

The Power of Delusion
Seriously considering limiting belief systems without also addressing the power of self-delusion is difficult to do, because these two roadblocks support one another. To minimize our cognitive dissonance (experiencing conflicting

beliefs simultaneously) we skew, twist, and delete information—all to attain internal comfort.

Delusion is subtle, which is why we are easily duped. A blatant lie is easy to see. But often something is true and the opposite could also be true, depending on the angle from which we view the matter. Many of our beliefs are half-truths. And how do we argue with a half-truth when it's what we want to believe?

To continue with the example above, Ted says to Jadon, "When I hear you making a pitch to our customer, I think you're a sleaze bucket." Jadon feels the knock to his sense of integrity and is tempted to point out all the times that he has acted with principle: he stood up to speak the truth even when it cost him dearly, and he does what he says he will and says what he does. Considering the examples in his own mind, his conclusion about being a person of integrity is fair. But that's not what the conflict is about. He's being confronted about how he sells products to customers. Prior to hearing Ted's challenging words, Jadon rated himself high on integrity. In staying with the challenge to his identity, Jadon must face the discrepancy between his view of himself and the view that his business partner and, possibly, his customers have of him. The value of that inner fight is in Jadon's facing who he is, bringing about a greater alignment between his self-perception and others' perceptions of him, *and*, as he makes even a small change (such as resolving to stop exaggerating the benefits of a product to pressure a customer to buy), earning more trust from Ted and his customers. The inner conflict has helped Ted be less self-deluded and attain better relationships.

Take another example of self-delusion: Claire is fearful that she won't measure up to the standard at work and says, "Management should be more humane—not all about numbers." Her annual performance review is one week away and her anxiety is mounting. It's true that management needs to think about people as its greatest resource but, once again, that fact obscures another: Claire has underperformed. Because deep down she questions her own adequacy, she tells colorful stories about when she was successful—and these are true stories. The other reality, which she doesn't acknowledge, is that at this point in her career she feels painfully unsuccessful.

All of us have a penchant for self-deception and are easily deluded. We have an uncanny attachment to our beliefs, regardless of whether they make us feel better or worse. Contrary evidence might be screaming in our face, yet we hold fast to our version of the story. An ex-husband says, "We're not done. I know she still loves me. Give her some time and she'll come back to me." However, the hard facts are that she moved on a long time ago and has made a new life for herself. By grasping the belief, he avoids facing himself, his fears, and his painful reality. Since we're not in the habit of questioning our concepts, we usually wait until someone else makes us confront self-deluded thinking. Maybe then we examine our delusions, explore the why of our beliefs, and potentially challenge them, thereby increasing our capacity to deal with reality as it is.

Guilt: the Deceiver

In addition to beliefs and self-delusion, guilt serves as another roadblock to seeing ourselves, because it readily deceives us. In my practice, I hear about guilt almost every week; we seem to trade in it quite regularly, as if it were common currency, but it's a tricky emotion. It often deflects us from the real issues and maintains our no-change position. Various aspects of guilt make it a stubborn roadblock, beginning with its power to anesthetize.

A powerful anesthetic. Guilt might just be the best anesthetic ever. Like a soporific drug, guilt is a potent sedative, numbing us to other emotional pain. And though we might not be fond of it, we would rather live with guilt than with the greater pain that it blocks. During surgery, anesthetics have the power to interrupt normal body functions for a time. Similarly, guilt blocks the usual pathways to the root of what's bothering us. We're okay with guilt because, for instance, if we were to acknowledge the anger beneath it, we might have to take action, and there is likely a part of us that resists doing that. Guilt, on the other hand, smooths over our inner conflict.

An easy companion. Guilt is a relatively comfortable long-term companion because it's so inoffensive to others (unlike anger or self-pity). Guilt doesn't hurt anyone. Rather, it points back to how you failed to make the mark. Feeling bad about yourself might make others feel better about themselves. People are okay with your guilt. If they are so inclined, they'll even support you and, in the process, feel good about their role. They are strong, encouraging, and compassionate. Over time, they may find your sense of guilt wearing, if it consumes your conversations, never changes, or if they must continually play the "helper" role. But for the most part, others don't become reactive around guilt—unless they're the ones making you feel guilty, and then it's a different conversation. Guilt is a tolerable emotion that maintains the status quo.

A relational lubricant. Guilt becomes a safe emotion when it acts as a lubricant in the service of relational harmony. You're not pointing at anyone else or asking anything from them. You take a one-down position as a preemptive strike—you'll take the hit before anyone can say anything (with the hope that your self-declaration will remove the other's need to shame you). External discomfort is at a minimum. You simplify your life by being in conflict only with yourself; it's more complicated to be in conflict with the other. Guilt becomes the cop-out: while you willfully accept full responsibility for something that went awry between you and the other, you bypass any potentially competitive dynamic. You safely assume a nonthreatening position because that is easier than facing your anger or having a difficult conversation about who is responsible for what. Though the relationship feels harmonious on the surface, both of you lose, because you've circumvented an opportunity for growth and deeper relationship.

An indicator of "goodness." The fact that we feel guilt also says something good about us. We put out a positive message, coupled with one of defeat, along the lines of, "I was bad but I really want to be good." Our guilt indicates that the other should not make conclusions about us based on our behavior. Rather, we want the other to know that our behavior makes us uncomfortable (and therefore we are still good). We have found a way to come out looking good and close the widening gap between what we think our bad behavior says about us and who we really want to believe we are. The internal conflict is quieted, at least temporarily.

A sticky emotion. Guilt is a puzzling emotion because although we say we don't like it, we're quite attached to it. We feel guilty when we don't really have anything to feel guilty about, and other times we behave in ways that we know will make us feel guilty. We often sustain it rather than ridding ourselves of it by acting.

Slippery forms of guilt. We hold on to an illegitimate sense of guilt because it protects us from more difficult matters. For example, Rhonedene feels guilty that she doesn't take better care of her mother, when, really, she's angry at her for being demanding and critical. Rhonedene focuses on the guilt because doing so allows her to avoid an emotionally demanding conversation.

There's also real guilt that is attached to actual offenses committed. When we've done something wrong, in many cases we focus on reducing the intensity of guilty sensations instead of changing the behavior that created the guilt in the first place. For example, if I've shamefully smeared someone behind her back, my mind might work overtime to justify, delude, or distract myself, or to find some potent "feel good" to take the edge off and lessen the guilt.

Sometimes we feel guilty because we *don't* feel remorseful when we believe we should (because we know we have acted contrary to our value system). Perhaps you've had an affair or have otherwise deliberately hurt the other and experience not an iota of shame. You feel strangely justified, and that induces guilt.

Other times, the guilt sticks because it fits, but we can't bring ourselves to attach the emotion to the thing that's causing it, attaching it instead to a lesser offense. For instance, Haley feels guilty about verbally attacking her sister and then not speaking to her for several years. However, the weightier object of guilt is that in her heart she knows that her father handed down a better financial deal to her than he did to her sister. She's complicit because she accepted the deal rather than advocating for something fairer for everyone involved; that's the guilt she doesn't want to face.

Suppose that all the efforts of mitigating guilt shift the focus just enough so that you aren't forced to address the behavior that created it in the first place. How long can you maintain real guilt, and at what cost? That depends on you. What is your value system? What does incongruence do to you? How much incongruence can you live with? How far down the path of darkness are you? What are the pressures brought to bear by your community, and will you use them to face yourself? What consequences and what choices will you be forced to make?

Costs of not addressing guilt. The costs of not addressing real guilt can be devastating. Some people erase the guilt by also ignoring their conscience or their sensibilities, and they fall into darkness. They no longer factor in the consequences of actions taken or weigh the actions against a compelling set of values. Somewhere in the gradual slipping, the mindless tripping, or the reckless plunging into darkness, the internal moral compass has been lost or discarded.

For others, the conscience stays alive with guilt plaguing the brain, creating far-reaching disturbances. We know what we have done. We have lied repeatedly when we value truth. We have betrayed our commitment to love and have cheated with another. We have not followed through with promises made, yet we long to be reliable. We say one thing and do another. Self-destructive acts are adopted to quell the internal noise in the soul and psyche. The self-destruction might take the form of drinking too much for too long, binge eating, self-punishing, or wilfully enduring unnecessary pain. Many guilt-producing acts are performed in secret, and maintaining the secret compromises health. When guilty acts accumulate, when exposure is feared, and when reckoning is imminent, some people are overtaken by mental instability. They can't inhabit their reality because it has become too stressful, and they cope by going crazy. Guilt is costly.

Our sense of identity is affected by genuine guilt, and it can take us to a reflective place where we say something like, "I am not okay with what I did," or "I don't like what my actions say about who I am." If we do things that don't fit with who we think we are, our internal dissonance is formidable. Consider actions taken in traumatic situations—in war zones or abusive homes—and the repercussions of those actions on identity. The guilt of perpetrators in such circumstances doesn't get the attention it deserves.

Genuine guilt shows up in remorse and aches for an accompanying act of restitution. A heartfelt emotion emanates from somewhere deep inside where we wail, "What have I done!" We feel our negative affect on the other such that our own legs give way, or our upper body falls forward, or another deeply felt physical response occurs. We wish we could take back our wrong, and we cannot, so we do everything in our power to right it. Rather than wallow in self-blame, we use our sorrow constructively, by taking action that leads toward healing—between us and the other, or simply within us.

If we listen, guilt also calls us back to ourselves. Real guilt is the by-product of betraying ourselves. It beckons us to align our actions with our values so that we can be a little more congruent. That is inner conflict at work.

We can use the inner conflict triggered by the situation to shift to life-giving beliefs, to see ourselves for who we are, and to address the deeper issue behind the guilt—all of which leads to increased freedom. Otherwise we maintain the pain at a chronic level.

So, What Now?

When conflict with the other creates conflict within, use this dynamic to challenge your beliefs, to break through self-delusions, and to face the real issue behind your guilt. Try the following:

- Use your next fight to find one belief that keeps you safe and also hems you in. Then question that belief, because it drives your behavior.

- Increase your self-awareness by inviting feedback from a boss, colleague, partner, friend, or family member. What does this person see about you that you don't see? Seriously consider all the feedback, even if you think it's only ten percent true. The act of questioning yourself is an antidote to self-delusion.

- Learn about your guilt. What is the difficult issue or emotion that your guilt shields you from? If you face that, then you can remove a roadblock and see yourself and the way ahead more clearly.

- Refuse to stop short at guilt. If you have committed an actual offense that warrants your guilt, what action could you take to make it right?

CHAPTER 13

Overcoming Self-Tripping

The benefit of engaging our inner conflict is that it enables us to overcome self-tripping—though addressing competing parts within is never a swift or simple task. Self-tripping behavior consists of those actions that create problems both for us and for others. Others have expectations of us that we strive to meet, but even more critical than failing to meet others' expectations is failure to meet our own expectations. And at the same time, we also depend on conflict about our self-tripping behavior to help us change it, though this dependency is mostly unconscious.

What behavior does the other not like in you, and what behavior do you not like in yourself? Do any of the following three examples ring true? Use them to stimulate your thinking about your self-tripping behavior:

- *Unreliability.* Roger doesn't want to be unreliable, but he leaves loose ends and doesn't follow through sufficiently in completing tasks. His partner is getting frustrated with him because he promises and doesn't deliver.

- *Uncontrolled anger.* Abigail "loses it" and her anger splatters like red paint on those around her. Later, she "mops up" the mess with profuse apologies and turns on her charm with a round of coffee for anyone within earshot. Unfortunately, her apologies are functionally hollow, because everyone expects another outburst again soon. She and those around her are losing patience with her short fuse.

- *Laziness.* As much as Leah wants to be disciplined, she can't seem to get off the couch and to the gym. Yet she can feel the unspoken expectations emanating from her roommate's judging eyes. She copes with his criticism and her own guilt by buying a new outfit to look good, reaching for a beer, or napping until the uncomfortable thought of her undisciplined nature disappears.

Maybe you are fully aware of your self-tripping behavior. You have named it and you make allowances for it. Maybe you are just slightly aware of your self-tripping behavior but haven't really faced it because of the discomfiting view of self that it creates. Or maybe you haven't even acknowledged its existence and aren't aware of its full impact on your life. Still, you have numerous personal strengths that offset your limitations. But the problem is that your self-tripping limits you and your effectiveness. It stands between you and what you really want—and perhaps it stands between you and your partner. Maybe you can feel your partner drifting and the vitality in your relationship waning. This is also unsettling. "Fine," you say, when the other confronts you with your behavior flaw. "Tell me something I don't know! The truth is that I feel helpless to change." Before thinking about engaging change, let's first honor where we are.

Changing the Behavior Involves More Than One Thing

If we feel bad about ourselves, why don't we do something about the bothersome behavior? Because that behavior is not just one thing. If fixing it were a matter of a single, isolated change, we would probably make it. Each behavior is held in place by something else, which makes change complex. Internal and external factors govern how we act. Some things we have more control over, some less, and some we believe we can't control at all, such as the other person's response. In constructing a self, we adapt to our environment and the relationships within it and, mostly without knowing, build the best structure we can within our limitations. Messing with the structure by pulling out a pillar or post destabilizes the whole thing.

Visualize a framed structure before it is covered over. We see how one two-by-four is nailed to another. We see the joists, the load-bearing walls, and how one piece of the frame supports another. In very concrete terms, we see the interconnection of each part to the whole structure. Once the structure is in place, if we should need to alter a critical post, how do we do so without destroying both that which supports it and that which conceals it? During house renovations, for example, think about how much drywall is sacrificed to deal with fundamental plumbing, electrical, or structural problems. We intend to make a cosmetic change, and then realize that there's rot behind the drywall, and now we're embarking on a much larger project than anticipated.

At the personal level, we know intuitively that one change in our behavior often introduces another and that this invites conflict on at least two levels. We experience *internal* conflict as the opposing parts of ourselves vie for dominance. For example, one part of us wants to assume the initiative, and the other part wants to be passive and let someone else take the lead. We also experience *external* conflict because someone close to us is invested in our staying the same—because although at one level the other wants us to change, if we do, they'll have to change as well, and they're not prepared for that. For example, if we decide to drive, the other might resist because they're not prepared to be a passenger. Their resistance will remind us why we didn't attempt a change earlier.

For all these reasons, many of us settle for living in a crooked edifice rather than repairing it; the process is too complicated, the task too daunting, and the consequences too severe. In the words of a client, "It's too hard to change the way you live your life." When we don't believe that we have what it takes to renovate our own internal structure, or that of our relationship, and at the same time we know that the framework can no longer hold itself together, total dejection sets in. Some people despair so utterly that they contemplate blowing up what they have built altogether.

Exercise: Examining the Behavior that Holds You Back

Here's a challenge. If you like it, do it; if it feels too much, skip it.

Take the form of self-tripping behavior that holds you back and examine it until you feel both tender- and hardy-hearted toward it. Think about a particular behavior that's causing difficulty within your marriage, for instance, or at work. We need that push from the other to face ourselves and change. Shake up the well-established, tightly fastened internal structure that supports this behavior with a series of questions:

- What is one behavior you do that you don't like?

- Why do you dislike this behavior?

- What do you like about this behavior, or why are you attached to it?

- If you tried to change it, what would you lose, or how would the change destabilize you (internally) or your relationship?

- What attempts do you make to mitigate the negative impact of your self-tripping?

- How is the self-tripping working for you?

- Is there anything else that holds the behavior in place?

- What kind of pressure is there from those around you to change the behavior?

Think about each question long enough to let it do its work within you. Don't settle for your first answer. Work on the premise that your first fifteen answers will be throwaways, because those answers are what you've been telling yourself for a long time—and they have kept you in the same place. Use your friends, spouse, or business partner to push you further as you explore a situation. Brainstorm, and produce as many answers to the questions as possible. Come back to them a day or a week later and keep adding to your answers until you find one that creates a significant shift within you. Let what the questions reveal surprise you, warm you, and make you squirm.

Nadia Tackles Negativity

Nadia's spouse and family describe her as being negative. Though she struggles with their description and wishes it were not true, she recognizes that there is some validity to their feedback. She can be moody and looks for something to make her happy. Others seem to delight in the nothingness of life—at least it seems to Nadia that their happiness has little to do with what's happening on the outside but appears to erupt from somewhere deep inside.

Rather than celebrating all that is good in her life, Nadia finds it easier to see the things that need to be improved. At times the darkness settles on her like a menacing cloud and she feels helpless to get out from under it.

Depression nastily grips her mind and soul. She wishes she had a different temperament.

Clearly Nadia must contend with the neurochemical cocktail she's been handed. That reality cannot be denied and needs to be factored in. But what else makes changing her negativity difficult? Numerous other compelling factors hold it in place. Here are her responses to the self-tripping behavior exercise above:

What is one behavior you do that you don't like?

- Be negative.

Why do you dislike this behavior?

- When I'm negative, people don't enjoy being with me. I want people to be with me because of the pleasure they get rather than out of a sense of obligation or duty or because they want to be supportive when they think I need it.

- I feel defective.

- Because I make myself unhappy.

- I'm not fun to be around and drag others down.

- I think my spouse is losing his affection for me.

- My spouse would rather go out with his friends than spend time with me.

What do you like about negativity, or why are you attached to it?

- It emerges most naturally. I see what is not or what could be.

- It's where I think I add value. I see some things others don't.

- Pointing out what is not quite right now is the best shot at having a better future. I don't want to be oblivious to what could improve because then the situation will remain as is.

- I trust it. It feels real and makes me feel grounded.

- The blissfully happy seem as if they're missing the stomach and stamina to face reality. They selectively avoid bits of information and situations that would rob them of happiness and they skate above what really is.

- I value critical thinking because of the vistas revealed and the choices created.

- It keeps the other attentive to me. They will continue to try to make me happy.

If you tried to change your negativity, what would you lose, or how would it destabilize you internally or your relationship?

- I would lose some power.

- I don't know if I could be anything else and still be me.

- My family expects this of me. Even when I'm not negative, they still see me this way.

- There are others who fill the uber-happy role.

- Being negative or critiquing or assessing is tied to holding on to a value system rather than being caught up in "anything goes."

- Being positive would eat up too much energy.

- I'm afraid to let go of the attention my negativity brings me.

What attempts do you make to mitigate the negative impact of your self-tripping?

- I put a positive spin on some things so that I don't drown in the negativity.

- I look for legitimate outlets for my negativity (for example, a career that values critiquing).

- I look for adrenaline hits (for example, intense exercise, food, exciting activities, engaging with people, sex, a good movie).

- I create meaning out of negativity (in other words, it's necessary to make me and others better people).

- I buy gifts to compensate for not being fun. At least I'm generous.

- I work hard at maintaining a nice home.

How is the negativity working for you?

- It is becoming unmanageable and growing at a faster pace than what is beneficial.

- It's starting to define me.

- Those around me are losing patience.

- It's negatively impacting my relationships.

Is there anything else that holds the negativity in place?

- I guess because I can, I get away with it.

- The long-suffering care and compassion of those around me.

- Negativity is a part of depression, which I believe is partly caused by my social needs not being sufficiently met. And cash is limited. Meeting my needs by getting out more will only increase tensions between me and my partner. With his resistance, I only question myself more and doubt that I have what it takes to go out on my own socially. I'm too serious.

- I don't have to change myself now. During the week, it's doable because I'm sufficiently distracted. I'll change it sometime in the future.

What kind of pressure is there from those around you to change the behavior?

- Perhaps there hasn't been enough outside pressure to necessitate change; my negativity has been tolerated. But that's changing.

- When I want to change, I get resistance from my partner and succumb to self-doubt instead of pursuing my social needs which might make me feel more optimistic.

Reading Nadia's example may be helpful, but you will gain more from doing the exercise yourself. And just as outside pressure spurred Nadia to rethink her self-tripping, so pressure from the other in your life—because they are tiring of the impact of your behavior on them—pushes you to consider change.

Take a moment to review your own answers to the questions. Again, this is a perfect time to ask for feedback from those who know you best. Are there self-delusions at play? Could you challenge any of your thinking? Might the opposite be true of any answers? For instance, in the example above, "Being positive would eat up too much energy" could be turned around: perhaps, in fact, it takes more energy for Nadia to hold on to her negativity than it would to think positively.

In any of your answers, does your thinking stop short and need to go one step further? For instance, Nadia might consider that the "uber-happy" role of others in her network could be their way of compensating for the impact of her negativity. What beliefs hold *you* hostage? When did you adopt them and for what reason? As you reflect on your own answers, do you notice any shifting within? After doing the exercise above, Nadia is no longer convinced that she "doesn't have what it takes." The self-limiting belief is softening. She also recognizes that some change on her part is necessary to safeguard her family relationships.

If you want to push further and possibly have a breakthrough, keep revisiting these questions to see what else they reveal. The deeper you go, the more the questions will help you work through the self-tripping behaviors that keep you stuck. Nadia's partner was losing patience and tensions were rising between them because of her negativity. Her fear of losing her partner's devotion helped her apply a hardy heart to the right fight—against the self-tripping behavior. As you unsettle your self-tripping behavior, can you feel its grip loosening a bit? What shift is emerging? Is there an action that now feels almost within reach?

This is not a simple process, and sometimes you'll fail despite your best intentions. Extend grace to yourself, because at least you're thinking about it.

So, What Now?

Capitalize on the energy of dissatisfaction for change. Use the conflict created within—when you don't meet your own expectations and feel pressed by the other's expectations of you—to change the behavior that trips you up. Try the following:

- Pay attention to the strain your behaviors create in your relationship.

- Name your limiting, troublesome behavior. What exactly do you do to sabotage your success?

- Instead of succumbing by simply coping or making excuses, this time take one little step toward overcoming the behavior and then enjoy how good a small victory feels.

CHAPTER 14

Navigating Unmet Expectations

The value of using the fight within when the other doesn't meet our expectations is that we learn we have options: we become aware of two separate roads and recognize that we don't need to go the route of demand and anger. Instead, we can discover our yearnings and address the fears behind our expectations. When we use the fight within, we're challenging ourselves to be the person we want to be, regardless of our circumstances. We recognize we have more control over the relationship than we thought we did, and we're able to stay connected even when the other doesn't meet our needs. A heart closed by resentment and bitterness can be replaced with an open one, full of warmth and compassion. That's the power of using the fight within—and the best-case scenario! *But* be prepared, because this road is tough, long, and lonely. Feelings will be intense and need to be fully acknowledged, experienced, and honored.

Decoding Expectations

Most conflict has something to do with unmet expectations; however, expectations are positive and essential—they're integral to who we are, relate to our goals in life, and are necessary when we work alongside one another. Expectations inform our present, shape our future, and pull us beyond the mediocre. They also help us prepare for what lies ahead. Expectations can be healthy, useful, and they are always informative.

They can also be problematic. For example, one of my daughters would certainly say that my expectations had created conflict between us. In my mind, we should have been conversing deeply or, at minimum, playing exciting games at family celebrations. I recall a pivotal moment while talking through that disappointment with my husband, Diet, when he said to me, "If you keep holding out for something that isn't, you're going to miss the good stuff that's right in front of you." Those were disturbing, sobering, and helpful words.

What makes expectations problematic? For starters, they are often anchored to a belief system that protects us from our fears—and from ourselves—at a deeper level. You'll notice how conflict keeps bringing us back to beliefs: we might hold on to our "shoulds"—what parents, children, weekends, and so on "should be". Though these concepts might be helpful at some level, if we become entrenched in defending them, we're prevented from facing what it says about us if our shoulds don't happen. And to avoid that further, we may pressure the other to comply to our shoulds, thus realizing our expectations. When the other thwarts us in our efforts, we might feel threatened and desperate, because when expectations aren't fulfilled, unwelcome identity issues emerge.

Expectations are intricately tied to our communities, whose contexts form the backdrop on which a life lived is cast for evaluation. Expectations relate to the question "What is normal?" Comparison is a natural way to determine the norm: "How does my family life, work life, or community life compare to others around me?" Expectations are about getting these things right, fitting in, and belonging—and therefore expectations directly impact identity. What do expectations, met or unmet, say about who we are?

I had an expectation that Diet would maintain a religious practice, attending church and so on—after all, we'd been doing that since the beginning of our relationship and it was integral to how we had come together. However, when his spiritual understandings shifted, some of his practices did too. In desperation, I tried to convince him to keep buying in to the old program—with many illegitimate means. There were times when I attempted to manipulate him so that he'd fulfill my "should," and other times that I assumed a victim role—though I didn't see it as clearly then. When I didn't get what I thought I needed, I became resentful and wanted to hold back from him something he needed. I made him pay for my pain in underhanded ways—passive-aggressively—by withholding social tidbits about friends though I knew he wanted me to share. I became bitter and hard inside. But I didn't like being that person either. The following diagram emerged from my struggle with unmet expectations and captures the choice—the two possible roads—that were in front of me.

For the rest of the chapter, we'll explore the journey down the two roads. If you're already capitalizing on the fight within, you might not be tempted by the slippery slope. Or you might find yourself on the slippery slope—because it feels effortless and intuitive—but since you already know that the end point will be massively dissatisfying, you might step off mid-way to embark on the hill with a view. Climbing this hill requires considerable fortitude, not only because it feels counterintuitive, but also because, at the bottom, the rewarding view is not within sight—and you aren't even sure there will be one. Yet this road holds infinite promise.

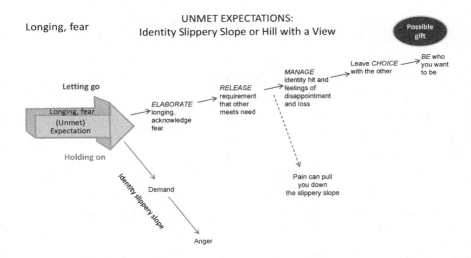

Slippery Slope

The road becomes a slippery slope because expectations quickly morph into demands. Once we have determined what *should* be, we also believe that we are entitled to it. What's the implication if we're living with more or less than the norm? For instance, think about people who read surveys about a population's frequency of sexual activity and place themselves on that continuum.

That information potentially impacts identity and can transmute into a compelling need. "I must have it," we might rationalize, otherwise "I am not desirable," or, "My life is less and therefore I am less." The expectations could become laser-focused and self-absorbing.

Where an expectation has morphed into a demand, anger and potential hostility are always close by. In desperation, we plummet down the slippery slope from what could be (our expectation) to what we cannot have and what we are not. We are likely filled with anger, or we plunge into despair. We can feel ourselves hardening to the other and to the situation and though we don't like it, we feel helpless to wrest ourselves from this state. The full-on fight (either internal or external) ensues.

Hill with a View

Expectations are too compelling to be silenced. They represent a form of energy that begs for an outlet. If we don't want our expectation to lead us down the slippery slope to hostility, then an expectation must be granted a legitimate voice. What are the yearnings, longings, and hopes that fuel the expectation? What fears lurk in there as well?

In my story above, I felt frantic because my comfortable world of certainty I had created was falling apart with Diet's decision to stop going to church. I remember sitting in the pew when Diet put his hand on my knee, looked into my eyes and said, "Unless you get a nail gun to hold my feet to the floor, I can no longer be here." We had always done things jointly. I didn't know if I would be able to hold my own socially and spiritually without him, or what would happen if we had a disagreement about fundamental values. Would he think I and my beliefs were flaky? Would his voice drown out mine in our children's ears? I longed to successfully pass on to my children the rich heritage of my past; to "get life right": and to enjoy the social outings afforded by the community, during which he had always been my fun-factor.

Expectations and their attendant, underlying fears and yearnings are hard to name. We need one another to help us see them. So, for now, maybe it's enough to recognize that our deep desires are the essence of what makes us distinctive. Can we make space for and become curious about them? Doing so creates a sense of vulnerability and softness within. Our yearnings encapsulate our core values—what we consider to be most important. When we elaborate on our longings, we make ourselves known to the other, and more known to ourselves.

We acquaint the other with who we are and what our need is—and here is the clincher—without necessarily requiring that the other meet that need. Releasing the other from meeting our need is a challenging part of this process. Previously we were holding on to the need with a clenched fist, and now we're not only unclenching but standing there with an open palm—not to let go the longing, but to let go the requirement that the other fulfill it.

What comes next is the most difficult part: we're moving toward core identity issues and our position feels tenuous at best. In releasing our expectations, we might be faced with being not enough, not having done it right, and so on. This is a tough place to land.

Feelings of sadness, disappointment, and a profound sense of loss surround us. We have no idea whether we'll get the thing we hold dear. A reflexive reaction at this stage is to remove ourselves from this vulnerable place by demanding, "This expectation must be met!" Yet this is the time we need to increase our tolerance for the difficult emotion so that we can move in a new direction.

Disappointment deserves some special attention, because we can easily get stuck in it. It seems that one major task in life is to learn to respond well to disappointment, a feeling we encounter from a young age. We might be enticed to set low expectations as a way of shielding ourselves from disappointment.

What might "responding well" to disappointment look like? We can't step around it because it won't let us. If we try to pretend we're not feeling it, it comes out in another form. Disappointment insists on being felt and acknowledged. As with any difficult emotion, the problem is not what we feel but what we refuse to feel. (For more information on emotional connection, Google "Raphael Cushnir").

For me, fully expressing the disappointment and sadness about Diet's decision to stop going to church—just being with the jumbled mess inside me—helped me carry on and afforded me some release. Disappointment guides us to important matters of the heart; it's too important to neglect. Use your disappointment to find the fears that hold you hostage and the yearnings that make you, you. Use your disappointment to fully acquaint yourself with your sense of loss. Plumb the losses until they reveal the illusions that feed them—for instance, that life should be a specific way, that the other should do a certain something or be a particular someone for you, that you need the other for something. (Recognizing my illusions about Diet was freeing for me. One illusion was that Diet should always be who he once was in our marriage. It's an impossible guarantee, an absurd hope.) Disappointment in times of conflict exposes our illusions and gives us an opportunity to free ourselves from them. But since shattering illusions can be arduous, we must expand our ability to soothe ourselves with anything that is calming, encouraging, and honest. We might encourage ourselves with statements such as, "This is tough, but I know I'll be okay"; "I'm going to go with *what is*, rather than fight my life"; or "I'm going to remain open and curious and see where this takes me."

If responding well to disappointment sounds too difficult, think about what happens when you grasp at what you think you or the other should be. Possibly, your eyes squint, your face muscles tighten, your stomach contracts … or you have another physical response typical in conflict. Frustration easily morphs into blaming others, disillusionment becomes encrusted in cynicism, and hopelessness gives way to bitterness.

If you can find the grace to let go of your requirement that the other meet your need, you give the other a choice. They have heard about what is important to you. Does it matter to them? If, over an extended period, the other shows they really don't care about what is important to you, you need to ask yourself why you are in the relationship, particularly if it's a primary relationship. What will the response of the other be to your expressed longing? Can they fulfill a need, or can't they? Would they be inauthentic if they did? And, if they can't fill that need, do they find another way to extend love and care? In my story, for example, Diet would meet me at the door when I came home from church, a wonderful spread on the table for lunch. If the other chooses to meet your desire then you'll get what you want. They give you a gift and you recognize it as such. If they choose not to, you are left with a substantial task that has a highly valuable return.

In a love, family, or friendship relationship, you understand the great undertaking of learning to love well, particularly when you don't get what you want. You must learn to love well *despite* your situation rather than *because* of your situation. In a work relationship, likewise, you get to be who or what you want to be precisely when your needs aren't met, and especially when the temptation is to stay angry and retaliate directly or indirectly. Personal transformation doesn't occur in one fell swoop; rather, evolution occurs during one small, seemingly insignificant incident after another. Each time you confront an unmet expectation, disappointment lurks.

Once you stay on track for even a few minutes and you've experienced loving well or being whom you want to be *in spite of* your disappointment, you crave to do it more, because it liberates you. The constriction you feel dissolves and you feel somewhat peaceful, even amid the unsettled state. The conditions are far from perfect but you feel lighter—much lighter. Releasing the expectation, or holding it lightly, is accompanied by a sense of softness rather than the rigid, hard state felt while hanging on.

Having let go the required expectation, you may be surprised by a gift that miraculously comes your way. At first you won't even recognize it as such, because the wrapping doesn't resemble anything you were on the lookout for. However, as you slowly unwrap it, or as it wraps itself around you, you will likely recognize this gift to be more valuable than what you sought in the first place. Perhaps you want compliance from the other. That's what I wanted from Diet, and getting it would have simplified matters considerably. But there was something bigger for me, just outside my field of vision: the real spiritual work of uncovering who I would become when my expectation was not met. I could keep acting badly out of hurt and fear, or choose to nurture an open and compassionate heart. A bonus was that Diet's uninvited challenge to my thinking contributed substantially to the depth of my spiritual viewpoint. For the two of us in our marriage, divergent thinking about significant matters creates a separation that feels healthy, though not always comfortable. The journey is strange. Sometimes what you get from the other is something you hadn't yet imagined, would never have asked for, and only in retrospect, often, do you see its value. We may not get what we want, but maybe we get what we need.

So, What Now?

When the other doesn't meet your expectations, focus on who you want to be instead of what you think you need, and discover your options. Try the following:

- Ask yourself what fear lies behind your expectations.

- Express your longings without requiring that the other meet them.

- Fully feel your disappointment and sadness, and find the illusions that feed them.

- Nurture an open heart of compassion, and refuse to feed resentment and bitterness.

- Be receptive to a surprising journey.

CHAPTER 15

No Longer Enabling the Other's Difficult Behavior

Another benefit of using the fight within is that we discover which difficult behaviors in the other upset us the most and why. We learn how we've sustained them. Our difficulty setting an external boundary with the other was because of our inability to set an internal boundary. Once we face what was holding us back and push through our limitation, we become clearer on what we can no longer tolerate, and we increase our options for responding to the other's difficult behavior.

The list of ever-troublesome behaviors is practically endless: inflated view of self, intimidation, bullying, irresponsibility, lying, duplicitousness, and passive-aggression are but a few. Any of these difficult behaviors readily pulls focus, affecting several people in the relationship system, sometimes even when the person is not physically present: "What will she think?"; "Will he be okay with this decision?" The puzzle of difficult behavior is that we give it—and the difficult person— power, by holding ourselves hostage with our own limitations. Consequently, we tolerate the difficult behavior. If we didn't abide it, it wouldn't be in our life. And note how much we can complain about what we tolerate.

The other's difficult behavior keeps us stuck for a couple of reasons:

- As much as we dislike the impact of the other's difficult behavior, it also keeps us in a comfort zone. Truly distressing behaviors legitimize our ignoring the role we play in a problematic dynamic.

- Certain difficult behaviors cause us to bump up against an inner limitation. This limitation prevents us from addressing the other's difficult behavior; it also inadvertently feeds the difficult behavior we want extinguished.

Difficult Behavior Pairings

In situations where the other's problematic behavior has become entrenched, often there's a corresponding behavior we're doing that inadvertently sustains it. This discussion explores how responses to difficult behavior, like the balancing of a teeter-totter, act to keep the behavior in place. Below are six examples of common pairings of difficult behavior. See if any of these resonate with the patterns in which you're caught:

Irresponsible and overly responsible. The overly responsible person holds out hope that the irresponsible one will step up and assume more responsibility. This classic pairing can be a source of ongoing struggle, with considerable push and pull, or an endless game of waiting for change, with diminishing hope. The cycle becomes self-reinforcing because each behavior sustains its opposite. Yet neither person is truly served by the implicit agreement. Realistically, letting go of overly responsible behavior is usually easier than attempting to shift irresponsible behavior. But that depends on if the overly responsible one can hold back instead of once more compensating for the other's lack of responsibility.

Selfishness and selflessness. In this pairing the selfless person has difficulty setting boundaries or standing up for self. Selfishness has a blinding quality that makes it hard for the person to see or admit their nature. When the selfish party gets away with being indulgent, they mistakenly believe that everything is as it should be. You'd think that selfishness would learn from the example of selflessness but, as careful observation reveals, that doesn't always happen.

Criticism and affirmation dependency. Criticism works because it matters to you what the other thinks. Perhaps you need them in some way to get by and don't feel sufficient on your own—you depend on their affirmation, so you take their criticism, hoping that the next comment they direct at you is praise.

Procrastination and too long-suffering or not long-suffering enough. Acting can be delayed because perhaps you are being too patient with the other, tolerating behavior longer than you should. The consequences of a task left undone might also be insufficient to change behavior. On the other hand, you might be too demanding—not long-suffering enough—and the other is procrastinating because they don't want to be told what to do. Procrastinating is a way to hold on to power when it's threatened.

Defensive behavior and judgmental behavior. When the other defends themselves, pointing out where they've got it wrong often feels necessary. At the same time, your judgmental behavior activates and feeds the other's defensiveness—a perfect pairing.

Verbal attacks and helplessness of a victim. This is a tragic pairing. The more the victim caves in to powerlessness, the more the abuser laces attacks with disdain and ridicule. The more the victim is diminished, the less they can break out of the destructive pattern. In such cases, the assistance of a third party is essential because the victim will be unable to shift the power imbalance on their own.

Although your response to the other's problematic behavior might inadvertently fuel it, there's no blame here. A pairing behavior is not responsible for, nor does it justify, the difficult one in any way. The key point is that though your corresponding behavior may make perfect sense, it does not serve to bring the difficult behavior to an end. This is where engaging your inner conflict is critical, because it can free you up enough internally to shift your relational dynamic.

Look for the hook that keeps you in this frustrating interactive dance. There must be a force at least equal to the frustration that keeps you in it. What's the significant struggle in your identity that locks you in to your pairing behavior? Getting unhooked requires surmounting that personal limitation.

Understanding How Identity Feeds Difficult Behavior

The expectations you have of yourself can lock you in to a track that narrows your options. Suppose you need to please people or to be seen as helpful or diplomatic (you are attached to an image of yourself). Maybe others have come to expect certain things from you because of how you've trained them to think of you. You are the accommodator, you're easygoing, or perhaps you're the person who always comes to the rescue.

The complexity of our internal system often works *against* change. One part of us prevents another part from making a shift. (See the Onion Skin Identity Model in Chapter 7.) Fear of the unwanted self (who we do *not* want to be) might make us invested in a persona (who we think we should be or who we want to be perceived as) in the community. The persona we project doesn't fit with the person we think we really are, but it gives us a payoff. Meanwhile, the kudos we receive for being a reliable contributor work against our being who we think we need to be at home. More times than we like, home gets the leftovers; we have little energy left to give because we've already offered ourselves generously in the community, and relinquishing the external validation seems too costly. After all, our sense of self is bolstered. Understandably, we get trapped in an identity struggle, unable to see our options. Let's consider two stories that demonstrate how this works.

Uri and Orville: An Irresponsible and Overly Responsible Pair

Uri is a director, skillful at off-loading his responsibilities to others. He's also good at taking the credit when others do well for him, and blaming them when they don't. As a manager who reports to Uri, Orville finds himself knee-deep in a bog of undone tasks. Orville takes on the role of being the ever-helpful assistant. When Uri under-functions, Orville provides the counterbalance. He becomes the overly responsible one who delivers. Orville gets saddled with more and more tasks, and though he's quite the donkey, he's beginning to sway under the strain. But he isn't one to give up quickly. When the going gets tough, he bears down, and his stamina is quite astounding. He also doesn't want to be perceived as a complainer and wants to avoid conflict.

Orville's expectation of himself is to be helpful, capable, and friendly, and he wants to be perceived as such. That's his persona. In his work community, he's known as the consummate dependable guy, loved by all.

What maintains the irresponsible and overly responsible pair, and what keeps Orville stuck? He gets accolades from his fellow employees. Most them are not fooled by the optics. They know his value and he feels appreciated. His behavior is being reinforced. In addition, in a tender, soft place at his core self, Orville questions his competencies. He believes that he must keep putting out in this manner because he doesn't have the same smarts as the other people on the team. He has opted to be the workhorse.

How can Orville extricate himself from this frustrating behavioral dance? Orville needs to face what he's running from, because whatever it is, it's limiting his behavioral options. His unwanted self is his self-perceived lack of smartness. He manages this by compensating and over-functions at many levels. This behavior works, to a degree, because he's fully appreciated and valued. Yet at the same time he has imprisoned himself because he can't stop over-functioning.

Coming to terms with his smartness, or lack thereof, could set him free. Perhaps he could say, "I really don't have to be as smart …" Or he could come to see the smarts that he's downplayed. If he embraces himself for who he is, then he has more options—though not necessarily easy ones, because he must give something up. He might feel freer to set boundaries, to say, "I can do this and I can't do that." By needing to be the yes-man and the agreeable assistant, he has made it possible for Uri to offload his responsibilities.

Complexity of the Internal System

Difficult behavior: Not responsible/under-functioning

Pairing behavior: Overly responsible

Role: The helpful assistant

Persona: Friendly, competent, nice

Unwanted self: I don't believe I can do anything else; I'm not as smart as the rest of the team.

Community view: The consummate, dependable person whom everyone loves

---

Craig and Adele: A Critical and Affirmation-Dependent Pair

Craig and Adele have been talking about doing house renovations for a while, but can't agree enough to move forward. Granted, the job involves some big-ticket items. Redoing the kitchen will necessitate a reconfiguration and a total remake of the cedar deck.

Craig is a highly capable and charming guy, full of great ideas. He takes a leadership role effortlessly. He's also a very busy man who runs out of energy by the end of the day. Adele is a capable partner who willingly carries her share of the responsibilities. Craig assigns tasks and Adele runs with them. She does the necessary research and just when she's ready to proceed with a decision, Craig holds up a stop sign. Once again, he is dissatisfied. "You should have thought about the color scheme," he might say. "The sequencing is all wrong." They reach a stalemate and can't move forward yet again. Adele feels bad not only because the job is stalled, but also because she has made numerous inquiries and now everyone is left hanging because of the couple's inability to make a decision.

What keeps them stuck? Initially Adele was feeling equipped and ready to execute the task. But with a steady stream of criticism from Craig, she's losing confidence. Adele now feels unable to make the decision and needs Craig's approval to act. She's sensitive to his left eyebrow, which moves crookedly, to the narrowing of his eyes, and to the sudden furrowing of his forehead. She longs for his affirmation and instead feels the weight of his disapproval on her. She hasn't met the standard.

Adele will do whatever is required to please him. Her role has always been the helper, and she is comfortable fulfilling it. Her expectation of herself is to be caring, kind, and giving, and she wants others to think of her in those terms. In the community, Adele expects herself to be a reliable doer, and over time she has trained people to expect that from her as well: dependable Adele. In moments like this, when she bumps up against Craig's criticism, she doubts herself. She hears herself thinking, "I can't," or "I don't know," and Adele is stuck. Their behavior pattern has brought their project to a standstill.

How do they extricate themselves from the pattern that keeps them stuck? Adele needs to find a way to realistically address her limiting "I can't." What can she do and what can't she do? She is skilled at doing the necessary research and has learned many things. In fact, in many areas she has more knowledge than Craig does. Will Adele be undone by Craig's criticism or can she find a way to believe in herself despite it? The truth is, if Adele moves forward without depending on Craig's approval, she will have some hurdles to overcome. There is no way that Adele can progress with the renovation project without making some critical mistakes. Working through the self-doubt and "I can't" will entail pushing past perfectionism and allowing herself to make some mistakes instead of quitting.

Complexity of the Internal System
Difficult behavior: Critical
Pairing behavior: Affirmation dependent—unable to make a decision without approval
Role: The helper
Persona: Caring, kind, giving
Unwanted self: I can't; I don't know (self-doubt).
Community view: The reliable one, a doer

If you adopt a new behavioral response to the problematic behavior of the other, that behavior won't automatically disappear, but at least you will no longer inadvertently be feeding it. Step back from your identity struggle by asking yourself a few questions:

- What limitations prevent you from reaching for your options?

- Are you being constrained by your unwanted self?

- Are you succumbing to self-doubt rather than feeding the wanted self?

Both Orville and Adele got stuck in a behavioral pattern because of internal roadblocks (Orville's was "I'm not smart enough," and Adele's was "I haven't got what it takes to make decisions on my own.") Those internal constraints led their behavior. Community and role identity were also potent forces for both Orville and Adele. Change is so difficult because one part of us fights against the other, while one part compensates for another. If Orville were no longer propelled by feeling not smart enough, he might say no to some of Uri's requests. His community identity might pay for it, if people no longer view him as the consummate helpful guy—which makes him feel good about himself. If Adele were to conquer the thought that she can't, she might shift the expectation of herself in certain contexts. As with Orville, there would be a social cost: she might no longer be seen as the caring, kind, and giving one. Instead she might develop a forceful, assertive edge.

Managing the effect of the other's difficult behavior is best accomplished by first working through the constraining beliefs and expectations we have of ourselves, so that we can freely choose behavioral responses that don't feed the difficult behavior. Using our inner conflict enables us to create a new pattern.

So, What Now?

Use the opportunity of the other's difficult behavior to confront the limitation holding you back from responding in a more helpful way. As you do so, the options for how to respond will increase and you'll no longer be feeding the other's behavior that you want extinguished. Consider the following:

- What's your internal roadblock? (It might be how you want to be seen.)

- Are some kudos from others possibly keeping you in a bind?

- Wrestle through the part of your identity that keeps you stuck so that you can experience more freedom in responding to the other's difficult behaviors.

CHAPTER 16
Breaking your Complicity

Often, we experience conflict in the context of a group or community—be it our family, friends, or colleagues. We might be an observer of tensions, or we might be in the center of them. Regardless of our position in relation to an existing conflict, we are affected to varying degrees, and that can create internal conflict. By using our fight within, we can break our complicity in the poor health of a conflict system. That will likely mean stepping up in a new way.

Take Ronald, for example. He marries Jazz, and by the time their third child arrives, his inner turmoil has reached peak levels. Jazz thinks Ronald's mother, Marylou, is a manipulative, controlling, and demanding so-and-so, and she doesn't want to go to family gatherings or invite the grandparents to visit with the grandchildren until Marylou changes her off-putting behavior. But Ronald, along with his siblings, has been inured to his mother's power. They accept that Marylou's a little dramatic, a little self-indulgent, must have her way, and doesn't take well to being challenged. But not Jazz. She wants Ronald to "man up," confront his mother, and support his new family.

Ronald, however, is not accustomed to challenging Marylou and identifies himself as a peacekeeper. Yet the more he tries to keep the peace between his mother and his wife, the more his conflict with his wife increases. "I'm not making excuses for her," he says. "I'm just trying to help you understand why my mother …" Ronald's voice trails off when he sees the condescending grimace flit across Jazz's face.

"You support her and not me," she says resentfully.

This pain has gone on for too long. To get through this conflict, Ronald will have to overcome some internal hurdles and find a way to assert himself with credibility and finesse. Though he thinks of himself as being the nice guy, respectful and dutiful, has also been known to lose his temper with his wife and others, which says (to me) that he has some energy and drive to work with. The pressure from his wife serves as the impetus to engage differently. Ronald is forced to access his strength within, get a handle on his anger, and develop the necessary skills to take a stand for himself and his family, or else he could lose his wife.

Amid his change, Jazz also has an opportunity to sort through her inner struggle. "Am I too demanding?" she asks herself. She doesn't want to be one of "those" wives. She wonders, "Are my expectations of Ronald and my in-laws realistic?" Jazz begins to question the longings and fear that drive her expectations. Two questions remain: How much outside pressure does Ronald need to face his internal struggle? and How willing is Jazz to continue applying pressure—or is she wearing out? As Jazz maintains her position and refuses the grandparents' access to the children, conflict heats up between Ronald's parents. Ronald's father begins to think he can't afford to be passive any longer, the cost has become too high, and he disagrees openly with Marylou. Ronald has never witnessed this before. The system is undergoing change because one person, Jazz, challenged the status quo.

Relational systems of which we're a part can produce great joy and, during conflict, considerable pain. Exclusion from a community can cause painful alienation. But belonging to a group can result in unwelcome pressures to conform, because each system—be it our family or friendship group, our workplace or our community group—is defined by its own structure, rules, norms, and behaviors. We feel the interconnection among all these when we move beyond the one-to-one relationship to multiple relationships within our system. Break an unspoken rule, and watch what happens relationally.

Ronald tried challenging his mother once and it devolved into a screaming match followed by a four-month break in contact. Take the risk of expressing a fuller, uncensored self, and we are quickly reminded of why we're conflict avoidant in the first place. When Jazz spoke up, she was snubbed by Marylou, who then began phoning Ronald at work instead of at home, which only promoted an unhealthy triangle. We know the consequences of speaking up and challenging the norms. This must be acknowledged at the outset, because breaking our complicity with the ill health in a relationship system is a substantial undertaking.

Yet the challenge in this chapter is to see if we can use our inner conflict to impact our relational system for good. Once more we are back to the conundrum of change—how can it happen? *The potential for change lies within the ongoing conflict between people who matter to one another.* Since significant conflict doesn't go away, and since we need or want to be in relationship with people, the relationship system itself, fortunately, helps us change by offering repeated opportunities.

When you feel yourself reacting in any one of your communities, pay attention to what exactly sets you on edge internally, because likely something is not as it should be. *Conflict simply highlights where something needs to change.* Use the inevitable tension within you and the system you're in to shift it to greater health—rather than simply managing the problem, which sometimes seems easier than making changes. Your inner tension is valuable energy to be harnessed for change.

The action you take is not neutral. Either it further entrenches the behavior and maintains the status quo, or your action moves the system in a different direction (even if the other stays the same), because you are changing. Because people are connected in a relational system, if you alone shift your behavior, others will be affected by your new stance and the opportunity for turning the system toward greater health exists. Negative actions, or lack of action, are just as reinforcing as positive ones. When you laugh at something destructive, you are saying it is okay. When you are silent, you withhold valuable input that could positively impact the conversational direction, and you let the dominant voices continue to carry disproportionate influence. In every action you take, you either discourage or encourage behavior. Which behavior do you want to encourage?

Possible Challenges While Using Our Inner Conflict

Numerous factors make shifting a relationship system toward greater health a difficult task. And it gets complicated because, rather than an objective observer, you are an "insider" and an integral part of the system. Yet by considering some of the possible challenges, you might have an even greater appreciation for what you can accomplish.

Our inner conflict has been dulled by the system. We've been swimming in our community pond for so long that, like the fish, we no longer see the water. We think that whatever happens is normal, because it has been our normal. The system has had its lulling effect on us and we no longer see what's really going on. (Drum roll, please.) Then enters a new family member—our sister's husband, our cousin's wife—the in-law joins us in the fish pond, sees with fresh eyes, and upsets the equilibrium in the system. Now suddenly "givens" are not quite so given. In-laws end up getting (undeserved) negative criticism simply because, by their presence and input, they have significantly challenged how the system works (at great cost to themselves). Naturally, many new influences challenge a system, not just in-laws. The challenge here is to take notice (rather than allow our senses to be dulled) and use our inner restlessness to become an advocate for positive change.

To fit in, we are tempted to deny our inner conflict. We make sacrifices to live in community. Perhaps we compromise, accommodate, and adapt to be accepted. To get along with everyone, we might factor in the givens. In family, we might simply accept that Mom plays the victim card, Dad is a control freak, and Simmy is a sensitive soul, easily offended. Or in the extended family, Aunt Maureen is known for abdicating responsibility. She never brings anything to the potluck. Or in our friendship group, it could be tempting to excuse offensive behavior, passing it off on too much drinking. Challenging any of these patterns might feel risky because this community is where some of our needs are met, yet still paying attention to our inner conflict is critical. When you don't fit the system, see it as an opportunity for change rather than simply trying to conform.

We recognize the possible consequences of leading out from our inner conflict. Perhaps you are counting the cost of a possible break in contact if you challenge the other, determining if you're prepared to live with that result. Being cut off, or cutting off another, are actions never to be taken lightly because they reverberate through the relationship system. Brothers, sisters, aunts, uncles, grandparents, old friends, and acquaintances functionally cease to exist.

This raises a question about when cutting someone off is healthy or unhealthy, to which there is no simple answer. If you break contact with the other because you don't want to deal with the inner conflict and simply want to blame them, then likely you're cutting them off unhealthily, maintaining the pain. Ironically, the goal of breaking contact is to get rid of the hurtful person, and yet they're influence is inadvertently kept alive, factoring large by their absence in social or familial circles. If you're blind to the role you play in the conflict, then cutting the other off might very well be unhealthy. (Most of us are more blind to ourselves than we think.)

However, suppose you are listening to your inner conflict and determine that you can no longer tolerate a certain behavior from the other. You have patiently, repeatedly, wisely, and carefully (okay, that's a lot to expect—just give it your best shot) confronted the other, but they are unwilling to take responsibility for their part of the problem. Perhaps they even aggressively maintain hurtful tactics, to the peril of all involved. How do you mitigate the personal damage to you and to the system at large? What do you do with a bad apple in the bushel? This calls for tough decisions. A break in contact, limited contact, or conditional contact are possible, healthy options.

During my early career, I probably believed too much in the goal of maintaining or resuming a relationship. Since that time, black-and-white scenarios have given way to rich tones of gray. Sometimes not being together is just as it should be. I have also come to see great value in spending time apart when the party breaking contact is clear about expectations, boundaries, and unacceptable behavior, *and* remains receptive to the offending party when that behavior changes. I have witnessed many wonderful stories of change. One such story is of Ryleigh, who said, "I can no longer play this role with my mother. I can no longer be a pleaser, nor can I tolerate her harsh, manipulative tactics. I've had a conversation with her and told her what the new rules are." This process involved breaking contact, having limited contact, and Ryleigh determining that her mother's behavior would always inform her next step. By listening to her inner conflict, Ryleigh found a new freedom for herself in that relationship, her mother began to slowly shift her behavior, her siblings spoke out in surprising, fresh ways, and greater health was introduced into the family system.

Encouragement to Press On

Recognize that inner conflict simply signals where something could be better than it is. Keeping the desired future in mind helps us overcome the cost of pressing on for change.

Using our inner conflict is easier one-on-one than in a group. A group has its own rules, expectations, values, and patterns, all of which keep it stable and make it resistant to change. In a family system, for instance, if we don't fall back into our role, someone else will try to push us into it. When we fight the unhealthy behaviors in the system, we don't know if others will support us. We might be ostracized for challenging the norm. This becomes only more difficult if we are already marginalized because of our political leanings, religious beliefs, sexual orientation, and so on.

Learning to navigate our way through the conflict system in a group is essential if we want to keep showing up for celebratory events (though we may decide that we *don't* want to). Sometimes the most we can do is be true to who we are and separate ourselves from unhealthy interaction as it is unfolding. We might be silent instead of piping up, or we might leave the room. Either of these actions will give others something substantial to bump up against. This is difficult, and if we do it, we can leave the gathering feeling satisfied that we accomplished a worthy goal. At another time, we might step out further.

When we meet one-on-one with a member of this same group, we might have different expectations of ourselves. We might take more risks, ask more questions, and challenge more. The other, removed from the pressure of the group, is different too. Together, you might reach an understanding that will serve you well the next time you're both in the group. Why not try a new way of interacting with an individual and see what little shifts you can make?

Playing nice is tiring. Playing nice means acting like everything's okay when it's not. Making nice means doing the work for true harmony, which means being honest when things aren't all right. Though often frightening, making nice is also invigorating and energizing. For example, a family celebration looms—you're preparing for a birthday dinner, gathering for a wedding, or spending time together at the cabin, and your anxiety is rising because you're imagining the mayhem to come. You might even be working behind the scenes to orchestrate a "happy event." Maybe you coach a family member, rig the timing, or mull over who should and shouldn't be invited (but worry that not extending an invitation threatens backlash too). You know the trouble spots and the trying people. You hope that this time everyone will "play nice" and it will be a good time for all. We're suckers for picture-perfect moments.

Sometimes the event is a comforting success. At times a gathering works because expectations have been adjusted and there is an acceptance that for now, considering the outstanding issues between family members, this is as good as it gets. However, if your habit is to act like everything's fine between you when it's not, then likely you feel happy to leave the obligatory get-together behind, because pretending just becomes too tiresome. Sometimes the most wearing thing in the system is not even the shenanigans but the faking of contentment and the holding out for the perfect picture, which clashes with the reality experienced. If "playing nice" makes you feel worn out, why not share that with others, working instead toward "making nice" with a respectful, curious, gritty, and sincere realism? That's what using your inner conflict to make a relationship system more authentic looks like.

The way change happens often defies common sense. A seemingly insignificant action might leverage profound change in a relational system. For example, a shy, thirteen-year-old granddaughter, Shelby, is a relatively silent bystander at most family gatherings. When she says to her parents, "I'm not going to Grandma and Grandpa's house today because I always come home with a stomach ache," it becomes clear that the ongoing and vicious attacks between her grandparents are causing Shelby a lot of anxiety. Her absence at the gathering galvanizes the actions of other family members who are also dissatisfied with the damning putdowns. One small stand by Shelby sets a course of actions in motion. Her absence has a large effect on a long-standing problem. Her grandparents recognize that unless they change their behavior, they might be alone at future celebrations. This story suggests that systems are highly responsive, which is encouraging. Use your inner fight to bring health to a relational system of which you are a part. Otherwise, accept your complicity in its ill health.

Challenging one relationship creates opportunity for change in several. Visualize a group, each person holding on to the string from a ball of yarn, the strand lengthening, connecting all as the ball is tossed, zigzagging around the room. Connections are the beauty of community. Recall Ronald and Jazz. The shift between them led to an upset between Ronald's father and mother, with the potential of creating a more equitable and helpful relationship. Ronald reinitiates a difficult conversation with his mother to see if he can manage his own emotions, regardless of how she behaves. Ronald's siblings begin a new conversation about their roles in the current family dynamic. This is the system at work. One upset gets considerable mileage because it reverberates through the system, creating the opportunity for healthier relationships elsewhere in the system. Watch for the rippling effect, and be encouraged and grateful.

Stepping Out of Unhelpful Patterns

Patterns of relating among family, friends, or colleagues form under implicit or explicit agreements. Though these patterns worked at one time, they may no longer function well in a current context. To break unhelpful patterns of relating is a good reason for a fight.

The list of potential patterns is long. You might feel like a bystander in some of the destructive modes you observe in a system, but recognize that being an onlooker might be your part in the pattern. Which patterns do you currently find disturbing in your relationships? Consider external patterns between you and the other, plus the internal ones that inform the arrangement between you. Here's a sampling of patterns:

- *Refusal to acknowledge wrongdoing and compulsion to apologize.* You notice that the other rarely acknowledges a wrong. You don't know if they really don't believe they've done anything wrong, or if they simply can't bring themselves to admit it publicly.

  You notice that you feel compelled to apologize because you just want to end the misery. You do what you normally do: you give in, or you give up something that's important to you—a perception or belief, value or a desire—because secretly you wonder if you have what it takes to argue the case. The other is so articulate and persuasive. Meanwhile, you can't help thinking that a successful outcome for you, this time, would be to not apologize, but you aren't sure you can live with the potential fallout. Consequently, you give a wide berth to the other; they have become accustomed to it, and the pattern persists.

- *Ignoring and making excuses.* You and your partner have a major altercation. Though you were called almost unspeakable names the day before, the next day your partner ignores the whole event, as though nothing significant transpired. This has been the pattern for longer than you care to remember. It causes you distress, but your anxiety only increases if you think about addressing the issue between you. What if you lose control of your anger and do something foolish? What if the other loses control of their anger again? So instead you follow the regular routine for de-stressing. You make allowances and excuses for the other's behavior, and your own. You write the argument off as caused by "a little too much drinking," and the pattern continues.

- *Outperforming and being addicted to praise.* You notice that you are an above average achiever. People say you outperform. You are hooked on this behavior because when you do it, the accolades fall like sweet rain droplets on parched ground. You volunteer your services and others come to expect it. For example, when you said no a couple of times, your father said, "You've changed," and your boss said, "Is something wrong?" You could tell they were not pleased. Their comments were just enough to suck you back into the same old pattern. Disappointment is not something you want to risk again.

Some of the patterns adopted may have been dictated originally by circumstance. For instance, as the youngest sibling you assumed the role that was left in the family. (Perhaps the other, your older sister, is reticent to give up the powerful position she secured for herself.) Or the position you accepted in relation to the other was an adaptation to the realities of your situation. Your sister or mother would become hysterical, or a partner would go silent for days if confronted directly, so you assumed the easier position, going along with things. Or maybe in your role at the office, you came in as the upstart who needed mentoring and that situation influenced the relational pattern that developed. Or perhaps the pattern you slipped into—being a pleaser, for instance—was the best fit for where you were in your development. You weren't quite ready to risk standing alone. The opportunity to change relationship systems happens when patterns begin to chafe you.

When patterns are coming to the end of their life cycle, one person feels the unease settling in more than the other. If you are more disenfranchised by an arrangement, the pattern will stop working for you first. The other is still shored up by your deference, has become reliant on it, and has developed a style of operating around it. But you have become increasingly aware of the cost to yourself. The pattern is holding you back. Or maybe you've grown beyond your position in the pattern because you have worked through your inner obstacles. In the past, you wanted and needed the other to "do for you," and now when they do, it feels as if they're taking something from you.

Forging new patterns in old relationships is no small feat, because to break one outside, you must break one inside too. For instance, your external pattern might be that the other makes the decisions and you go along with them, if reluctantly; you might complain about a decision, but ultimately you don't change the pattern even though you don't like it. You are held hostage by an internal pattern that feeds the external one: when you feel anxious, uncertain, and lacking in confidence, you let the other take responsibility, protecting yourself from making a bad decision.

Another possibility is that an external pattern feeds an internal one: suppose the other usually makes a solid case for their way and gets what they want, and they cannot help but question your know-how if you make a decision. Your insecurity about decision-making is exacerbated by the other's questioning of your ability.

Sometimes your growth leads you to feel irritated by a behavioral pattern with the other, and you push for change because you can no longer tolerate the status quo. Other times, the other can't abide your behavior anymore and an ensuing fight triggers your inner conflict, which you can use to break free from a limiting internal pattern. The system is working. You nudge each other in the direction of greater health by refusing to remain in dysfunctional patterns.

Expect some resistance as you push for change, because the likelihood is high that the solution to your problem creates a difficulty for someone else in the system. (For example, Ronald's solution created problems for his mother.) Suppose that you want to become more assertive. You're bothered by being less than you are and can be. Yet the other finds you easier to get along with when you're more passive. Or suppose you want to be less controlling, but the other still wants you to take charge so that they can keep depending on you. Maybe you're ready to give up being the victim, but the other feels better about themselves when they can rescue you, or vice versa. In each case, resistance from the other forces you to examine how the problem is fueled and reinforced—and you gain an even greater appreciation for the difficulty of change.

In most cases, resistance will greet your "solution" to a problem because someone in the system thinks they benefit by keeping things the way they are, though their intransigence might be unconscious for the most part. It's not that the other doesn't want to be healthy or have a balanced relationship, but they're blinded by fears of loss and change, and they hold on to what they know, because uncertainty only heightens fear. The health of the system depends on the member who's being chafed pressing on for the desired change and not capitulating to the other's pressure to maintain what is.

At this juncture, a belief worth contemplating is, "What is healthy, good, and right for one person, is healthy, good, and right for the other, even when the change feels uncomfortable." (A caveat, though, is that we don't always know what is healthy, good, and right for us.) The system makes noise even when it moves toward increased health, and setbacks are normal.

The statement "I want to make a difference" has almost become cliché. Yet it remains a worthy longing of the heart. Here's the challenge: Why not make a difference right now, in the very community in which you find yourself. Doing so entails being involved and connected, so that you can have influence, and also being sufficiently detached to hold your own? Your inner conflict is highly valuable and not something to be suppressed, because it helps you break your complicity and promote health in the relationship system. Know that there is power in one. Conflict turns on one person.

So, What Now?

When you use the tension you feel within to courageously and sensitively address what's not working in your relational community, you help shift the system to greater health, and everyone benefits. Try the following:

- Pay attention to what upsets you internally, because inner and outer conflict signals the need for a change.

- Step up in way you haven't previously.

- Recognize that no action is neutral: silence and inaction often maintain the status quo.

- Step out of one unhealthy outside pattern by breaking one pattern inside.

- Applaud yourself for a small change made, because one small change begets another.

CHAPTER 17

Valuing Relationship Tension

Having gone within, we experience a new appreciation for the messiness of relationship and are hopefully more accepting of what the journey brings. We recognize that the struggle with the other helps us comprehend what's going on inside us. At the same time, we see that addressing our inner struggle helps us in relationship—the *raison d'être* for journeying deeper into self. In this chapter, we'll consider six realities to understand why tension is valuable.

The Gift of Feedback

Working with countless individuals over many years has taught me that we don't get the feedback we need. Employers let employees go without offering them the critical information that could help them at their next job. Family members choose to reduce contact with each other rather than speak up about what's causing the distance. Friends make excuses and indirect, disparaging comments before they address why being together is difficult. But that's because giving feedback is incredibly hard—a factor that needs to be appreciated more.

When we offer feedback, we're sharing our experience of the other, so it raises the difficulty we have with ourselves. Giving feedback requires vulnerability and feels risky. How well do we know ourselves? In addition, we're likely proffering feedback at a time when we're already experiencing some tension in the relationship, and we're concerned about the negative impact our words might have.

We often want to avoid giving feedback because it's intense, dicey work. It requires skill, and paying attention to the other's patterns and tying specific terms to their situation so that the information is understandable to them. (We can hardly do that for ourselves.) We're not sure how to say it or of the damage that might follow. For the feedback to be helpful we need to keep their best interest in mind, but sometimes we just want to get something off our chest because their behavior negatively affects us. Being encouraging and forthright when the message itself is disheartening is not a task we take on lightly. It's easy to feel that the timing isn't right, that we've said enough, that the other will figure it out, or that it's not our job.

Considering the difficulty of the task, if someone invests in us by revealing to us what we need to see, hopefully we'll recognize the value of their gift. Without feedback, we are vulnerable to self-delusion, because our brains are programed to reinforce who we think we are. We can only become aware of our self-delusion when we are informed and influenced by another perspective. We are dependent on the other for that.

Hurting Is Necessary

When we address the fight within, we recognize that hurting is part of healthy relationship, because to be "unhurtable" means that nothing can get to us. Knowing this, however, doesn't remove the sting. Hurting another can be subtle or blatant, calculating or candid, expected or completely unanticipated, malicious or well-intentioned. Regardless of how it's meted out, hurting cuts a slice.

But it's not desirable to be impervious to the comments of others. Suppose we could smack our lips with a deep-down satisfaction of being utterly pleased with ourselves and that complete self-contentment weren't a pleasure we hold lightly, ever so grateful for its fleeting presence. If this were so, we'd lose one of the best human qualities—soulfulness. Soulfulness is fundamental to connecting with each other around the human condition. If we weren't deeply stirred by life's events and interactions, then what would happen to our spirit?

If we shut down *hurt,* have we not also shut down *relationship health?* Letting stuff penetrate and stick is critical to the change process. The ability to empathize with others is most efficiently acquired by harnessing our own experiences of suffering. Understanding hurt can quickly build bridges to the other. If our need for empathy evaporates, how much compassion for the other dissipates as well? Letting ourselves feel allows us to also sense the other, and a human connection is created.

Relationships: As Fragile as They Are Hardy

Our experience in conflict helps us accept that relationships are both fragile and hardy—and that we're never quite sure what they can withstand.

A hardy relationship braves challenge: disagreement is an opportunity rather than a threat; conversation flows freely without undue censoring because we know the other won't take unnecessary offense; we prod the edges as opposed to erring on the side of caution. A fragile relationship, on the other hand, is delicate and easily broken. In such a relationship, veils, filters, and obscuring layers are the order of the day. We keep many and often the most important things inside, because, frankly, we don't trust revealing them. Withholding is defensive on two fronts: we don't know what the other will do, nor what we'll do when we state our minds. The outcome is uncertain. A relationship characterized by limited transparency becomes thin and shallow.

How freely do you want to speak with each other and how much do you want to hold back? A business partnership group I know agreed on a ten percent rule, meaning they would speak the whole truth, including the last ten percent of it. Sounds like an admirable goal. Compare that to the percentage you would consider for your intimate relationships. Perhaps the percent you hold back is higher than you'd like. Then again, after the fact, sometimes you're grateful that you kept your mouth shut. Perhaps the jury is still out on the ten percent rule.

As much as we want a hardy relationship, the truth may be that all relationships, from casual to the most intimate, are fragile. There are just too many variables. Every relationship is forever on the move as new seasons of life come and go, ushering in more change. Add the fact that we have no control over how the other will hear or interpret what we say. They are operating within a different context than our own.

Trust itself is a delicate thing because it's never static. We don't build trust and then rest in a dreamland atop some lovely pillow. If we've managed to build trust in a relationship, we operate from a strong base that enables us to take increased relational risks. Nonetheless, trust is highly dynamic and vulnerable to the impact of everyday events. "I trusted you yesterday. Do I still trust you today? Well, that all depends on whether you give me reason to trust you still."

Identity Shifts Slowly

Addressing our identity struggle within helps us to be realistic about the slow pace at which identity shifts. Also, identity doesn't shift in a vacuum, and often depends on a push from the outside. We don't change something until we face it, and pressure from outside helps us do that. Though identity shifts, it doesn't do so easily and is quite resistant to change. For one, those around us are not quick to let go of their perceptions. If you've been working hard at making a change, notice how long others take to become aware of it. We'll likely have to make an announcement that we're not behaving the way we used to, because the other will still expect the same behavior long after it's gone. For instance, if you have a track record of saying no, the other will operate as though the word has already left your lips, even if it hasn't entered your brain this time around. Just as it takes the other considerable time to see us differently, developing a fresh perspective about ourselves also takes time, with numerous repetitions reinforcing new behavior.

Fight Is Positive

Though nothing will remove the difficulty of a fight with the other, when we've used it to make changes, we come to see it as being positive and necessary. It's the impetus to surrender to what we've been fending off, so that we can find relief. Without the fight, sensitivities would fester instead of heal, the unwanted parts of self would become entrenched rather than transformed, and self-doubt would grow instead of becoming our growing edge.

As much as we want to change, we are hard pressed to do it on our own. Three factors help us overcome the inertia. One: when the consequences of our actions become intolerable, we become willing to embark on a change program. For instance, for many, losing relationships with children or grandchildren is motivation to do things differently. Two: considering our imminent mortality often inspires a shift in perspective—the impossible starts to seem possible. Forgiveness, for example, is asked for or granted and relationships are restored. And three: opening to love is perhaps the most powerful tool for overcoming stagnation. Who really knows what love is? How do we describe it? Maybe we don't have to. Maybe it's enough to view love through a pragmatic lens, because we see what happens when this ephemeral quality is in play. If there is a threat of losing the love we value, we suddenly become capable of actions previously unthinkable. Love has the power to move us and our encrusted souls, sometimes this way and sometimes that, no way altogether pure or perfect. Yet when love moves us, significant things happen, and change has a chance. That is the power of love.

More Fleeting Than We Like

In our attempt to use the fight for change, we acknowledge with all humility that our gains are sometimes fleeting. What about when going within doesn't work? We have taken the journey deeply inward and discovered some freeing insights. We may have experienced an epiphany of sorts; maybe we see something about ourselves that previously we didn't, and we say, "I get it." Then we wake up the next morning and wonder what "it" was. Or we begin to see our situation in a new light, and then the fog covers our revelation. The insights gained are more transitory than we'd like. This is the case for Bakari, whose story illustrates how tenuous realizations can be.

The epiphany for Bakari is that he is holding out for the leadership position in the family business for the wrong reasons: he wants to prove to himself and others that he's capable and he wants the status that comes with leading a successful business. But, truth be told, every weekend, Monday looms like a dark cloud on the horizon. He doesn't get excited about his work and feels like he's often teetering on the edge of his competency. He acknowledges that volunteering for a nonprofit youth organization is what really fires him up. In a quiet, restful place inside, he believes that he needs to look for a career in the helping profession. When he faces what he really wants and who he really is, he feels aligned inside.

But when Bakari walks into the bustling family office, the urgency of the day takes over and clouds the clarity of his epiphany. Once again, he's seduced by the carrot of being the owner of a growing company. Bakari has been expecting to fill this position for as long as he can remember, and he thinks this also fits with his parents' expectations. When things are not coming together easily in his workplace, he just tries a little harder and tells himself that, in a matter of time, everyone will see he's ready for the promotion. Bakari's earlier epiphany faces some compelling and competing forces, inside and out.

Even though an epiphany might be fleeting, we've experienced it. And even if we don't remember exactly *what* it was, we will likely remember what we *felt* at the time. Perhaps when we saw something new about ourselves, or made a connection between previously disconnected parts, we felt more relaxed, open, and hopeful. Reimagine how you felt during that freeing realization, and commit yourself to returning to it.

Both fracturing and healing happen in relationship. Prior to using the fight to go within you may have thought, "How dare the other push my buttons," as though the person should know better and not do that. Yet at this juncture you might be surprised to see that incident as a potential moment for further healing of your sensitivity. There is a new acceptance for the messiness that relationship brings because it is pivotal to and necessary for personal health, growth, and healing.

So, What Now?

Reflect on what you have gained through the relationship struggle with the other. How have you grown, what have you learned, and in what area of your life do you now experience more peace? Try the following:

- Reflect seriously on the feedback that makes you squirm and use it to make a change. Perhaps you'd like to thank the person who willingly bore the cost of giving you the gift of feedback.

- Accept being hurt as an inevitable part of the relationship journey, and use your understanding of hurt to connect with others.

- Recognize that relationships are both fragile and hardy, and share of yourself in a way that builds trust.

- Be patient with yourself and the other, because shifting your identity takes time and repeated practice.

- Use the fight to make a change, and when you do, the fight will have positive value.

- Return to what you *felt* when you had your freeing self-realization, because epiphanies can be fleeting.

- Be encouraged, because the restless parts of yourself find peace through wrestling with others.

PART 5
ENGAGING THE OTHER DIFFERENTLY

You re-enter the fray intent on doing conflict differently, regardless of what the other is doing. Yet the paradox is that, to practice a new way of relating to yourself, you need to interact with the other. The old traps are still close by and repeated efforts are required to engage the other in a new way. You might be surprised by how difficult this process is, but you will also be delighted by how freeing it is when you succeed. Your unilateral changes yield nourishing benefits.

CHAPTER 18

Fostering Curiosity About the Other's Perspective

Turning the lens on our inner self was for re-engaging the other and/or the world differently (and feeling good about ourselves in the process). Going back into the fray contradicts our natural tendency to remove ourselves from the challenge to our sensitivities. But returning to the fight with the other is an opportunity to solidify the gains made by our personal work. The healing of our sensitivity takes root in the context of the other.

In the presence of the person who previously undid you, see if you can maintain a sense of well-being, if only for seconds or minutes. Acknowledge to yourself that this person may always have an unusual or special ability to unsettle you, but at least your feeling of "undoneness" will decrease. Becoming curious about the other's perspective is key to engaging them differently. Yet inviting the other's perspective might even feel dangerous in various ways.

The Danger of the Other's Perspective

As you think just now about the other's perspective, reflect on a personal conflict story, one you create about *you* (and the other), and notice how it both serves and keeps you stuck. (Remember that your opponent, meanwhile, is constructing a different version of the same event. Take a moment to consider their possible rendition and the impact of your behavior on them.) What is your specific attachment to your story? What has the story given you? How does it make you feel about yourself? How does that story also keep you stuck? What would you lose if you loosened your grip on your own story and added the other's story?

Danger in hearing it. When our identity has been negatively implicated, seriously considering the other's perspective might feel dangerous, because our view of self is at risk. For instance, perhaps you believe that you contributed substantially to your company's growth, but your boss views your contribution as minimal. That direct hit to your self-identity forces you to rethink how you evaluate yourself if you want to get through the conflict.

The other's perspective potentially alters your story significantly. Yet you are quite attached to your version because it serves you well on several fronts. Your story may have helped to contain overwhelming confusion and out-of-control feelings. It gave you just enough understanding of what was going on between you and the other to bring some personal relief. With the information you had, you made your conclusions. Wouldn't messing with that story now catapult you right back into the old feelings you tried to escape in the first place?

Sometimes the danger in listening to the other's perspective is that you'll lose your own. It might be swallowed up entirely or become diluted. Or maybe the issue is too important to risk finding any middle ground. Maybe you can't afford to listen to the other's perspective because you've done that too much in the past. Possibly you fear that if you hear the other's perspective, you will once more cave in and not get what you really want.

Your version of what has happened between you and the other most likely makes you look like the better one and the other appear worse. Creating a story that makes us feel better about ourselves is a simple reflex, because we're programmed for self-preservation, reaching homeostasis by finding ways to decrease our anxiety. Thinking of ourselves as the villain feels unnatural and may cause us to lose a valued role. Perhaps we have garnered support and brought others onside by being the victim rather than the persecutor.

Entertaining the other's perspective is dangerous also because something changes inside us when we try to get inside the other's head. From their vantage point, we see things differently—what they might require of us and are not sure we're ready to give it to them. It might be viewing the other in a new light, seeing ourselves differently, or telling alternative stories. The change might involve facing a fear or trying something we haven't tried before. Now what? Where to?

Danger in obliterating it. The consequence of obliterating the other's perspective is true danger. We insist on being right, even when we're wrong, making everything we see and hear further corroboration of our story. Perhaps our love for being right is so strong that we would rather live in delusion than be wrong. At an ancient, primal level, maybe needing to be right is distantly connected to the need to survive. If we think our identity is being threatened, we fight to be right because to be otherwise makes us feel insignificant. We can hold on to being right, but if we're wrong, unfortunately, we'll demonstrate that—at least in this instance—we really are inadequate.

Consider the reverse scenario as well. If, in your situation, you repeatedly give in to being wrong when you're not, individual and relational health dictates that you can't afford to any longer. Holding on to being right is a necessary, and healthy, departure from an unhealthy pattern. Otherwise you end up being less than you are.

Another danger in expunging the other's viewpoint is that we may then settle for believing only one perspective, which will be a half-truth. Even if we don't necessarily agree with the other's framing, maybe we see how their story makes sense, given the angle from which they view the conflict. In trying to see things their way, we might recognize a misunderstanding between us, or gain additional information that casts the incident in a new light. A combination of their perspective and ours might be closer to the truth. Maybe we're more culpable than we imagined. Viewing only half the picture obscures fifty percent of our options.

Not hearing the other's perspective also creates a stalemate. One of the major complaints amid conflict is, "I don't feel heard." Under such conditions, headway stalls as a person makes the same point repeatedly. Perversely, truly considering the other's perspective can also create an impasse, because, at least for a time, new information increases ambiguity about what your next step should be. Perhaps the confusion leaves room for a third solution that contains both viewpoints to emerge.

On a global scale, denying the other's perspective contributes to some of the major conflict in our world. With our primitive brain's fear propelling us, the other becomes the enemy. We keep the story alive with a belief system that legitimizes almost any action we want to take. We are embedded in a tale of us-versus-them—this is who we are and that is who they are—and the stereotypes become entrenched. In casting the other as the enemy, we fool ourselves into believing that we've decreased our own anxiety and boosted our safety and security. Yet the sense of comfort is nothing but a veneer, and underneath the tensions fester, breeding only more insecurity.

Surprising security and safety in the other's perspective. What parades as safety might not be that at all. Guarding against the difference we don't understand (whether in a person or an ethnic, political, or religious group) feels safe temporarily, because to really engage with difference feels scary. Yet protecting ourselves from the other also *increases* fear, anxiety, and insecurity, because these feelings multiply when they're not confronted. If we can approach the perceived threat to self, we might develop a greater sense of personal security.

When the other knows we are attempting to truly understand their perspective, perceiving us as an enemy becomes difficult, because suddenly they experience us on their side, if only for a moment. As we empathize with the other's perspective, they begin to de-escalate and their negative emotion diminishes. They're also more likely to be open to hearing *our* perspective. We have increased safety.

Three Tasks to Help You Cross Over to the Other's Perspective

As you assume the following three tasks to help you develop a greater appreciation for the other's perspective, you might envision crossing a bridge from one side to the other. As structures of beauty and intrigue, bridges evoke positive emotion and take you to remarkable places.

Calming Ole Iggy (the amygdala). When the amygdala is in overdrive, crossing over to the other's perspective is virtually impossible. We need empathy to enter the other person's headspace. The first task in traversing the distance is soothing the amygdala so it no longer dominates the neocortex. The language we adopt at this stage is critical, because it shapes our reality. We might tell Ole Iggy about the benefits of the altercation, the revelations that could emerge from this. We might remind ourselves that although we feel attacked by the other's words, there's a good chance this is not about us at all but about what the other person does when feeling threatened. We might coach ourselves for endurance with a statement like, "This difficulty is time limited."

Looking at yourself. Taking a good look at the darker parts of ourselves changes the way we see the other, because it provides us with a deeper respect for the invisible complexities that propel all behavior. Knowing our shadow doesn't make the other's poor behavior legitimate, but it makes demonizing the other more difficult. Harsher judgment gives way to some understanding, or even compassion, because we realize that each of us is struggling with our own gremlins.

Adopting the belief that there must be an explanation. What would happen relationally if each time you were caught off guard by something, your first response was, "There must be an explanation." You might now be thinking, "That is just Pollyannaish, feeble thinking for people who don't have stomach enough to digest the grit."

Alternatively, you could assume that the other makes sense, just as you do. This isn't psychoanalyzing the other but expanding your understanding of them, because even when people say or do seemingly stupid, destructive things, there's a high likelihood the illegitimate behavior came from a legitimate need. This doesn't excuse anything, nor does it absolve them of responsibility for their behavior, but it activates your curiosity and tempers your judgmental reflex. It also provides another avenue of exploration: "Why"—this three-letter word not only serves as a promising gateway to new discoveries, but it shifts you from the reactive brain to the rational neocortex. "Why would they say this? Where was that coming from?" Such questions open you to learning about the other.

The most significant matters about the other may never be revealed to us, but at least we can operate as if the invisible exists. We recognize that the most pertinent matters that impact everything are those we're not privy to. We give the other the benefit of the doubt and recognize that their story has validity even though we don't fully understand or necessarily agree with it.

Seeing You

When parting ways, "See you," are words that slip off the tongue unthinkingly, because they're a customary farewell. But how much do we really *see* the other? In South Africa, Zulu greetings contain rich, honoring subtleties. *Ngibona* says, "I see you as a person"; *Ngikhona* means, "I am here." The response to this greeting is, "Until you see me and I acknowledge your greeting, I do not exist." This is in keeping with *Umuntu ngumuntu ngabantu,* which means, "A person is a person through other people." Our identity is based on respect and acknowledgement from others. That's a weighty condition in the context of conflict, and it makes our internal and relational struggle understandable in the first place: our interrelatedness causes a dependency that creates vulnerability. To be unseen is contrary to a fundamental human hunger. Being seen, on the other hand, creates a potent sense of acknowledgement that affirms, "I am," "You are," and "We are one when we are two." That is relationally profound.

The words "I see you," each pregnant with meaning, are potent.

- I see *you.* You are different than I am. Right now, I let myself fade into the background and you are the main character on the stage. I see you separately from how your life impacts, intersects, or interacts with mine. As much as possible, I remove myself from the equation so that this really is about you.

- I *see* you, really see you. I see you when you speak to me, and I see how you speak to me. I see your intensity and understand what you're saying is important to you. In your reactivity, I see your fear and know I have activated a sore spot. I see your eyes well up and am privileged to witness that which moves you. I see the harshness in your face melt into tenderness, or the other way around. I see that when you pause, you're struggling to speak, holding back, or putting on your happy face with, "Everything's fine." I see when you keep silent. I see how hard you fight for your voice to be heard and how quickly you give up. I see beyond what you express and wonder what's not been communicated. I glimpse your internal spirit from which all these things emanate.

- *I* have crossed the bridge to your side of the divide to see the view from your vantage point. I come to this interaction with you, bringing all that I am, with my own hang-ups, limitations, and shortsightedness.

I see you is my attempt to understand who you really are with a refusal to stop short at my own understanding. Once I really see you for who you are, I will interact with you differently.

When we're realistic about what lies ahead, as we are heading back into the fray to engage the other more successfully, it's natural to feel hesitant. We won't get it right immediately, nor do we need to. We can be satisfied that we are still trying. I am frequently astounded at the boundless effort clients, and all of us, expend to achieve better relationships. That's got be worth something.

So, What Now?

Foster curiosity about the other's perspective, because that's the key to engaging them differently. Hearing the other's perspective is not simply about saying the right things. It is *feeling into* the other's experience. When you empathize with the other, the conflict naturally begins to de-escalate. Try the following:

- Start by believing that the other makes sense and then set out to discover how.

- Find the legitimate need beneath their illegitimate behavior.

- Let the three-letter word "why" work for you, or adopt an attitude of wanting (or needing) to hear more.

- Ask the other the simple questions that you forget to ask when Ole Iggy dominates: What do *you* think? How do *you* see it? What do *you* want? What are *you* feeling?

- Recognize that in crossing the bridge to engage the other's perspective, the way you see the problem might be altered forever. You won't seem as right, the other won't seem as bad, and the situation won't seem as clear.

CHAPTER 19
Doing It: Engaging Differently

By now you have probably spent considerable time pondering your sensitivities, exploring how they impact your identity, and learning about how they make you vulnerable to the other. But since recognition and insight without *action* results in personal disillusionment and possible contempt from the other, experiment now with interacting differently, precisely when your buttons are pushed: you re-enter a situation in which you had difficulty with the other and the feeling of being undone or out of control is still fresh in your memory. You might re-engage voluntarily, curious to see if you can hold your own this time. Or you might suddenly find yourself in a familiar, fraught situation and must scramble for a new way to act instead of reverting to frustrating patterns. This chapter will help you pinpoint the moments when you can bring about change in your circumstance.

The Old Pattern Stops with You

At this stage, you're no longer feeding the cycle. As you move from the old to the new, the other will still likely play to your sensitivities; this defensive behavior worked for them in the past, but now a noticeable change emerges. Your reactivity has decreased. Shining the light on the conflict and a commitment to stay the course help you break the pattern.

Shining the light. One helpful technique amid a repetitive cycle is to shine the light on what the other is doing or what's happening between you. With your reactivity decreased and your heart rate at its almost normal rhythm, you are more capable of seeing and hearing clearly. To gain perspective, you can step outside the interaction momentarily and look in with a third observing eye.

"Shining the light" on what the other is doing is not to shame or humiliate them but simply to highlight the dynamic in the moment. For instance, you might verbalize, "That's a put-down"; "Right now you're giving me the cold shoulder"; "It's happening again—we're doing the same things that get us nowhere"; or "Are you trying to make me feel bad right now?" Naturally, the tone and heart in what you say is highly significant. (These are not statements of attack; rather they are meant to expose and to reflect the immediacy of what occurs between you.) They are not guaranteed to turn the situation around just yet, but they can signal a halt. In that moment, you have illuminated *what is*, and the other can look at themselves. If you're fortunate, they will be at least a little uncomfortable with being that person you've identified, and the interactions might veer in a better direction. On the other hand, they might feel rather stupid and try to re-establish their footing by upping the ante and doubling the hurtful behavior. So be prepared for that.

Staying the course. Regardless of the other's response, your task is to hold firm and refuse to get caught in the same hopeless patterns. The undertaking may be more difficult than you anticipate and you might be tempted to quit, particularly when the other ramps up their tactics, sustaining the shenanigans for much longer than you think you can bear. Vulnerable to the same triggers, you might get pulled in like before, but you remember what it felt like to be free for even a few moments. Remaining unhooked for several seconds or minutes is success, even if you are caught again later. Next time you might be able to stretch to five or ten minutes.

Moving on Unilaterally

A common belief that unnecessarily restrains people is that it's not possible to move forward unless the other is also willing to take a positive step. This is wrong. Make your move independently of what the other is doing or not doing. You are back to being *who you really want to be*. What action on your part will make you sleep comfortably in your own skin? Looking directly at your own stuff has released you and created a new sense of freedom within, even if only for snippets of time. With every reaction, the other unwittingly reveals more of themselves to you, and you become a little clearer on the action required.

When they're angry, for instance, perhaps you will no longer let the anger shut you down, beat you up inside, or cause you to lash out in retaliation. Or when you get the silent treatment, rather than letting it hold you hostage, you might call it for what it is and then set out to have a good day. When the other is negative, you might refuse to let it engulf you and instead find a sense of calm despite the situation. In circumstances such as these, differentiation can serve you well (see Chapter 21). The other's behavior no longer destabilizes you like it once did.

Less Reactivity Is Not About "Anything Goes"
Decreased reactivity on your part, and increased understanding of the other's perspective, does not diminish your standards about what is acceptable and unacceptable. When your thinking apparatus is functioning well, you're clear about what you are and are not willing to live with. This position arises not from desperation but from quiet, firm knowing. You speak with credibility and the other takes notice. In fact, they experience begrudging respect for you. They are experiencing your healthy pushback, simply by your being fully you.

You're likely saying little about the other, although your comments reflect on them in some way. Your words are about you as you declare yourself and make your truth known—which leaves little to argue with. You might say, "I can't let myself be pushed around by your anger anymore"; "I can no longer afford to be shut down by your tears"; "I want to be with a partner who's sexually intimate"; "I am unwilling to be held hostage to this stalemate"; "My passivity doesn't work for me anymore"; or "I can't absorb nastiness anymore."

You have probably heard someone say, or have said yourself, "You can't change the other person." Clearly, the statement holds some truth, but it's not the whole truth. Since you operate within a contained system—as a couple, for instance—if you change, the other cannot be the same. You change the other by changing yourself.

Even while living with the reality of your change, the other still might not change. If they don't, then more definitive and possibly radical moves are on the horizon for you. You have been clear about what you need, what you can tolerate, and what no longer works for you. If the other cannot engage differently, then you must take the course of action that's right for you.

Let's examine some tools for changing the patterns of relating between you and the other.

Interrupting Cycles and Breaking Patterns

During conflict, there are at least three crucial ways you can consciously engage differently: change your behavior, attend to your unwanted self, and wrestle through your self-doubt. Pay attention to when you lose your personal power.

Change Your Behavior

Controlling feelings is hard to do, but we can control our behavior, albeit with a struggle. Sometimes we forget that. If you think you can't control your behavior, reflect on how you might feel similarly in situations at home and at work, but at work you won't let yourself lose your cool with the boss because you can't afford to be fired. In contrast, at home, you might let it rip because you can. Suppose you adopt the belief that you can control your behavior. How might that belief interrupt a vicious cycle?

When you feel threatened, what damaging behavior do you reflexively adopt? Is your tendency to act out, or to hold back? Consider the following:

- If your tendency is to act immediately, do you say or do things that inflict damage? If so, then next time you might decide to restrain yourself for at least twenty minutes and do nothing. Spend a few minutes by yourself in another room, step outside for some fresh air, or go for a brisk walk (sometimes you need a physical outlet that matches the intensity of your internal energy). If you think that writing a letter will result in a better outcome, then do that. Personal reflection gives you time to cool down. These are all good strategies.

- If, on the other hand, your tendency is to take no action, you might decide that this time you need to engage sooner. You can't afford to wait twenty minutes because withdrawing only invites more attack. The other needs a response.

Is changing your behavior possible without addressing the pain driving it? Change can be ushered in through various gateways. Why not go for what's easiest in each moment? (Note: Sometimes behavior is the most difficult thing to change.) By changing behavior, you might work backward and forward simultaneously, looking afresh at what you used to feel and creating new feelings as you act differently. It might also be that when you see the other respond favorably to your changed behavior, you are encouraged to keep the good will in play. Remember that each of you is continuously shaping the interaction—your last action informs the other's next action, and so on. While you recognize your interdependence, being mindful of your independence is important. You can determine your course despite the other's behavior. If you can find the grace to interact respectfully, particularly when the other is behaving badly, the cycle begins to shift significantly.

Attend to Your Unwanted Self
The unwanted self brings you to the heart of the pain. Understand how and where you can engage differently by exploring the five possible actions below.

Accept needs not met. Part of what keeps us stuck in the conflict cycle is that the other holds the keys (that we've given to them) to something that we believe we need or want. Needing and not getting from the other has left us vulnerable. We are desperate for them to make us feel okay about who we are. That isn't what we say to ourselves, but it is what fuels conflict. Accepting that our needs will not currently be met by the other motivates us to be who we want to be so that we can give ourselves the reassurance we crave.

Refuse desperate acts. When we don't get reassurance, a sense of desperation sets in. In desperation, we adopt behaviors that only make things worse. Now we really are who we don't want to be. We lash out or go cold and become unlovable or unlikable, making it easy for others to reject or disapprove of us. Instead of giving in to your desperation, turn to healthy, self-soothing actions.

Loosen your grip. At this point, staying overly attached to the other is too costly. The other is in no position to give you what you need. Loosen your grip and pull back. Your sense of self is too important to lay it at the mercy of another. Turn instead to the question, "What do *I* think of me?"

View the other as separate from you. You have cut a cord, at least temporarily, and you now likely see the other as quite separate from you. You see that their hurtful behavior is not only in response to your behavior, it is also a reflection of their own internal struggle. Instead of writing them off, you enlarge your perspective of what's going on for them and between you. You are detached and simultaneously you recognize your dependence on their feedback because it still informs what you think about yourself.

Take a moment to self-reflect. Once more you are back to the question, "What do I think about me?" Am I lovable (or worthy, or acceptable, or smart, and so on)? The difficulty of this question is partly in its timing. There are many times when you feel wonderfully lovable, but you're asking yourself this question when you feel lacking. You must answer the question on your own, despite what you think the other thinks about you. You look at it realistically: "When am I lovable?" "When do I become unlovable?" and "What action will I take right now so that I feel more lovable?" The change comes when you lovingly and truthfully take care of the restless part of your identity by proactively being who you want to be in the *here and now.*

Wrestle through Self-Doubt

Self-doubt raises numerous unsettling questions. For example, "Have I got what it takes?" and "Where am I lacking?" The upside is that change has the best chance in times of uncertainty. The moment self-doubt is magnified it has the potential to shrink.

If we give in to being less than we are or can be, long-term romantic relationships can be a breeding ground for self-doubt. Deferring to the other because of their capability in a certain area results in our own capability remaining underdeveloped. Or we might expand our capabilities and then back down when we experience some form of resistance from the other. Possibly the other likes being in charge; is convincing about the way things should be done; is charismatic, winsome, or forceful. Letting them take control is easier than learning to fly ourselves. Self-confidence gets pummeled, to be replaced by self-doubt.

In whatever context we're in, whether encouraging or discouraging, we must be open to the person with whom we're doing life in tandem. The other might have something to say that we need to hear, something we have not considered, are not prepared for, or are not being realistic about. We hold their voice in tension with ours, allowing the two voices to wrestle. "What is legitimate?" "What is the truth about me?" We are simultaneously receptive and discerning. We also wonder about where their voice is coming from. Why are they saying what they do? Are their best interests served by keeping us on edge? Do we see their tactics for what they are? They may want to keep us in the same place because that's less unsettling for *them*. If we are not discerning, we might miss what is really going on between us and the other.

Wrestling with self-doubt requires listening to your own voice. If that's your challenge, how do you turn up your own volume? That depends on both of you. If the other is particularly forceful, you may have to increase the force of your own voice, not necessarily with its volume but by speaking steadfastly. Or you might ask the other to ease up, if they're receptive to that. You might need to get some physical space so that you can center yourself. That could range from turning your back momentarily (as an act of turning toward yourself), to temporarily going to another room or taking a time out. You might have to block the other in your mind, as though erecting a wall, to reinstate balance. You might mentally step back to recapture the clarity of vision you had at the outset of the conversation and just hold yourself there for a bit.

Self-doubt is pivotal for leveraging change. Either we cave in to it or wrestle our way out. The next time you bump up against the wall you can't get past, what if you stay for a while and push past the point when, ordinarily, you'd quit? There's a good chance you'll have to overcome fear of a consequence that until now you have not wanted to live with. If you can move through this familiar place where you usually come to a halt, then the cycle can no longer be the same and your options increase.

Pamela Changes Patterns

Pamela finds herself again in a familiar position. Interactions with powerful people cause her to shrink and go silent. This time the situation is with her sister Petri, but other times it's with Peggy, her colleague, or with Pierre, her boyfriend. Petri waxes on about her ideas of how Mom's seventieth birthday should be celebrated. Petri knows the best caterers in town, the best musicians, who should speak and who should not and who should be invited. Pamela argues with Petri silently to herself, "Are you kidding me? You want to invite everyone that has ever brushed sleeves with Mom. This is ridiculous. Why do you have to be so pushy and forceful!" Pamela knows that when she feels threatened, her usual response is to shut down, nod, and escape as quickly as she can. She protects herself so the other can't get to her. She then limits contact for as long as the other will tolerate it.

This time Pamela wants to respond differently and push past the place where normally she stalls. Yet the very thought causes her adrenaline to soar. Her heart feels like a pounding drum, her face like a burning coal, and her extremities like fluttering, falling leaves. Her sister is a force to be reckoned with, but Pamela refuses to withdraw this time. She gathers all the internal strength she can muster and begins to speak.

As Pamela steps up to the challenge, her inner turmoil multiplies on several fronts. Fear and self-doubt grip her. She thinks, "Will it come out all wrong? Will I know what to say?" Strangely, her words are coming out with strength and conviction. This frightens her too. What if she will be perceived as a bitch? Pamela vowed long ago not to fall into a pattern similar to her sister's. But there's a double bind: if Pamela keeps her important thoughts inside, she can't help but be bitchy on the outside, because her voice needs an outlet.

When Pamela courageously suggests a more intimate event with fewer people, less fan-fare, and less show, she gets exactly what she anticipated from Petri: ugly resistance. Petri becomes forceful in making her case and slips in an undermining jab. "Well, you've never really known how to chitchat with people anyway." The shot is effective. Pamela knows that she gets tongue-tied with strangers and can't wax eloquent like Petri. But luckily, Pamela's no longer running from this truth. In fact, she's accepted that social banter is not her strong suit. When she doesn't need to defend herself, a new thought sneaks up on her. She has always been wowed by Petri's incredible schmoozing abilities, but what if the behavior is driven by Petri's need to prove something to herself or others?

As Pamela stands back to self-reflect, she gains a little perspective. Maybe her fear of being a bitch paralyzes her tongue in these pesky situations. Pamela begins to seriously reconsider her fear of being a bitch. Maybe there are times when she needs to be a little bitchy. Or maybe she can find a way of saying what she needs to say without being "a bitch".

Pamela takes a stand again, ready to speak up and see if she can hold her own with Petri another time. She comes up with a plan whereby they might get some information from Mom to find out what she really wants, while keeping the event a surprise. The proposal is a gamble, but it could just work. Petri is taken aback with the resolute tone of Pamela's voice. Petri eases up a bit. Pamela's voice falters and she blushes, "I don't want to sound like a bitch."

"Hey, I never knew that you felt this strongly about stuff," says Petri. A significant shift is occurring. Pamela is pushing past her limitations. The truth is that Pamela has the warmest and most caring heart and she also has compelling convictions that cry for an outlet, beg to be shared. If she can't grant herself a voice, maybe she will be destined to be a bitch. As Pamela speaks up, she makes valuable contributions and Petri gains an equal companion who carries the load with her. The old relational pattern between them begins to loosen, and they start down an uncharted path.

This is just one story of change. As you re-engage with *your* other, go for the change that fits. That might be changing behavior, attending to your unwanted self, or wrestling with your self-doubt. Think small. One small change begets another. The best part is that you can make these changes unilaterally. This is your commitment to yourself, not to the other, and yet the other also benefits.

So, What Now?

When you no longer feed the destructive pattern between you and the other, the vicious cycle slowly starves. Focusing on three manageable ways to change helps you engage the other differently. Try the following:

- Act in ways that will make you feel good about who you are. What's the one behavior change you want to make in your next pesky interchange?

- Attend to your unwanted self by coming back to the question, "What do I think about me?" Be who you want to be in that moment. Let that be your focus.

- Refuse to cave in to self-doubt and instead wrestle through by pushing past where ordinarily you would quit. In what ways do you want to trust yourself more?

CHAPTER 20

The Realities of Moving
Through Conflict

At this stage in the journey, allow your neocortex to work for you by saying things to yourself that will ground you and maintain your sense of control, rather than feel like you are at the mercy of the other. As you experiment with new ways, be realistic about what moving through the conflict will require from you. Now, let's explore the inevitabilities of slippage, the need for repetition, maintaining healthy pressure, getting back on track with each other, and the muddy business of apologies.

Inevitability of Slippage

Old patterns are automatic, exert a powerful grip, and pull you back with the force of a magnet. Be prepared for slippage, otherwise you'll be discouraged when it happens. You'll end up being hard on yourself for once again doing the same old thing, and you may be tempted to write off the other because they too revert to old patterns. Such behavior substantiates your fear that people really don't change. Here are some tips to keep in mind as you negotiate conflict with fresh eyes.

Be realistic about what you can accomplish. Establishing new responses in conflict might require numerous interactions. Rest assured that you are making progress even if you recognize an old pattern after the fact, call it for what it is, and resolve to behave differently next time. Next time you might catch the behavior while you're doing it; soon after, you might nip it right *before* you act. If you can honor your own meandering change process, you will likely extend patience to the other as well.

Have a clear, simple, and limited focus to guide you. To make the change manageable, decide on taking one action. Maybe you aim to keep your mouth shut longer, or speak sooner, listen rather than defend yourself, stay engaged rather than walk out of the room, come back to apologize, or refuse to raise your voice. If you do that one thing for even a few seconds more than you could do before, you'll have had a success. In those fleeting moments, you'll experience what interacting differently is like, which might be payoff enough to commit to a new direction.

Be ready to forgive yourself. Slippage sneaks up on you. Just when you think you've arrived in a better place, the other makes a gaffe and you feel ambushed by the old habits and pitfalls. That certain someone slips in an offensive dig and you feel slighted. You're struggling with your own identity again. The longer the other keeps up their destructive antics, the harder it is for you to sustain your change. You might also feel better about your interaction in the moment than you do in retrospect, when you see the slippage more clearly, or vice versa. But forgive yourself, because you're developing new internal and external patterns—and that's no easy feat.

Applaud yourself for what you did differently. One method for conditioning behavior is to reward any move in the right direction. After you recognize your change, you might want to announce to the other that you acted differently this time. This may seem strange, but your old response is so deeply etched in the mind of the other that they will think you're still doing your habitual response long after you've stopped. That's when a question like, "When is the last time you saw me do that?" makes an impact, because the other might be surprised at their inability to produce the evidence (and a new pattern between you is beginning). Hopefully a taste of the new and a glimpse of what is possible prevents you from chronically slipping back to the old pattern.

The Need for Repetition

Repetition is necessary to break old patterns. As the saying goes, "Old habits die hard"—really hard. To your surprise and disappointment, an old reaction might resurface even after years of lying dormant. Who knows how long it really takes to break a habit and adopt a new one? Twenty-one days is often touted, but for what particular routine, and under what conditions? This number must vary. What we do know is that breaking patterns requires repetition. That knowledge will have to assuage our discouragement when we suffer slippage as we try to change.

Maintaining Healthy Pressure

As with repetition, maintaining healthy pressure is essential to establishing new patterns between you and the other. You do this not by foisting something on to the other but by standing firm in your newly held position. At the same time, recognize that with increased pressure from you, the other will amplify the behavior that achieved results in the past, not because they liked the outcome, but because in desperate times we lapse into the behavior we know. Their ramped-up behavior probably will activate your own self-doubt again. But by now you're able to observe this taking place, as if you were standing outside yourself. Wrestle through your self-doubt by holding on to what you know is true for you and refusing to succumb to the tactics of the other that push you back into a place of confusion.

The inevitability of slippage, the need for repetition, and maintaining healthy pressure are important considerations when moving through conflict. Let's consider the hesitancy around resuming the relationship after noteworthy conflict.

Getting Back on Track after Conflict

You might get back on track with the other, or you might not. If you do, then you may initiate contact watchfully, see the "same old" in a new way, and find a friendly witness to help you along the way. You also might involve yourself in the muddy business of apologies.

Not getting back on track. Sometimes, when obstacles remain, *not* resuming a relationship after it has been fractured is the right thing to do. Perhaps one party is unwilling to re-engage. Or you may have finally managed to extricate yourself from an unhealthy situation, and you need to keep distance. You might also be up against a personality disorder and, regardless of how hard you have tried to work with and through a situation, a necessary change is simply not forthcoming. You determine that investing energy in the relationship is too damaging to yourself.

If you can accept the inherent value of the other without hating them and still part ways, that might be good enough. You've come a distance and know this position is the healthiest option for you. You didn't get the feel-good finish you were hoping for, but what you do get is adequate. Instead of feeling churned up as you were in the conflict, you're feeling relatively peaceful about who you were in the interactions between you.

Note: Don't be seduced into breaking contact as an easy way out if the situation doesn't call for it. Seeking input from those who know us well, and are possibly affected by our actions, can help us discern the healthiest level of contact for now, while we remain open to the winds of change.

Initiating contact watchfully. During past conflict, you may have staked your ground and acted adversarial because of a need to protect yourself. You were closed off to the other. Getting back on track is about the tentative and ever-so-gentle movement toward the other—if you determine that's a healthy option at this juncture. You are attentive, more receptive, and you look for openings with the other. Making the first move is difficult; you might speak a kind word, or not at all. You might offer a lingering look, a tender touch, an act of kindness, or an attempt at humor. Alternatively, the first move might involve meeting physical needs, such as offering to pick up a coffee or another such nicety. After emerging from a raw experience, a kind gesture is like the warmth of a fireplace on a cold day, even though it may also be received hesitantly.

Seeing the "same old" in a new way. Because you now embrace your unwanted self, you're less reactive, you hear and see the other differently, and are likely more aware of your triggers in real time. These triggers sent you running in the first place, but encountering them this time *feels* brand-new. During a conflict, you can sit back and say, "I see it, I get it," without having a fight-or-flight or freeze response. You just acknowledge what's happening. You see the rapid cycling of the reinforcing loop between you and the other. Although you're back to being in a conflict that's about both of you, you could not have learned to observe the dynamics without first removing your attention from the other to yourself instead. Having embraced your sensitivity, you see more clearly than ever before what the other does to undo you. You see your interaction in neon lights, and for the moment, just seeing that might be enough.

Finding a friendly witness. Repositioning yourself in the relationship can feel like a daunting task, because both the other and the external system want to hold you in the same place you've been in. Also, something in your internal system fights against interacting differently. This is when you need a friendly witness who shores you up when your resolve flags. Look for this person somewhere in your support network. When you lose your way, your friendly witness reminds you of what you saw before and what you know is still true. When you are confused, your friendly witness helps you simplify complex matters. When you are scattered, your friendly witness gently nudges you to refocus. When you make excuses or allowances for the other's behavior because you want to take the easy way out, your friendly witness holds you accountable—and not just once or twice: the friendly witness cares enough to keep bringing you back to your objective. This is the beauty of community.

The Muddy Business of Apologies
Apologies are another significant part of resuming the relationship once it's been fractured. "I deserve an apology," or "I'll have nothing to do with her again until she apologizes for what she said," are statements we have said, heard, or been told. The impenetrable wall goes up and we wait for action from the other. We'll now explore the muddy business of apologies, including what to do when a heartfelt apology is not forthcoming, dual perspectives and liberating powers, and missing the target and hitting the mark.

Aching for an apology. When we ache for an apology, we want recognition from the other that something hurtful occurred, otherwise we wonder whether they're oblivious to it. And we want to know, does it matter to them that they hurt us, and do they regret it? We yearn for the deep-down apology with which the other shows us they've wrestled with the action that caused the offense, because that offers the most hope for changed behavior. Given such an apology, we have reason to gradually shed our protective garb and be reservedly receptive to trusting the other again. Though an apology is focused on the past, its concern is really the future. We don't want this damaging thing to happen again.

How effective is an apology? Apologies can be viewed on a continuum: from highly effective, to adequate, to insultingly injurious. When does an apology do harm? What if we are simply trying to get the other off our back and settle things quickly? A matter of the heart has just been reduced to a tactical manoeuvre. In effect, the apology becomes a double hurt because it circumvents the difficult conversation that would tackle the real issues. Instead, the apology is used to smooth them over. To avoid perpetuating hurt, make sure your own apologies are genuine, not stopgap measures.

Apologies are tricky. The right words sometimes disguise a hidden state of the heart, even to the person uttering the apology. Faith communities are particularly vulnerable and susceptible to this kind of injury because of the mandate to forgive. To be virtuous, members reach for the gold standard of forgiveness, though the heart lags. They may be tempted to leapfrog over the anger and difficult conversations to miraculously land on forgiveness.

The situation could look something like this: Isaac comes to Abe and says, "I've struggled for quite some time to look at you or be in the same room as you. But I want you to know that I've forgiven you."

Abe responds with, "Whoa—sounds like we need to have a conversation."

Isaac says, "That's for another time," and blocks any further attempts by Abe to continue the conversation.

This apology is an insulting injury. Prior to the apology, Abe had no idea about Isaac's feelings. Now he knows of an intense struggle, and Abe has no recourse to deal with the situation. Isaac, on the other hand, walks away feeling like a good person who did the right thing. This is not helpful. Rather it is cowardly and hurtful. The more constructive course of action would have been for Isaac to courageously address what created the intense feelings in the first place. In such a conversation, Isaac and Abe would have learned more about themselves and each other, and sustainable change would have had a greater chance.

Does the apology hit the mark? The effectiveness of an apology is correlated to how detailed and meaningful it is. Apologies come in various forms; "I'm sorry," end of story. That apology might have some value, but the situation remains unsettled, because what exactly is the person apologizing sorry for? Here's another type of apology: "For everything that I (knowingly or unknowingly) did, I'm sorry." Covering all the bases, this apology throws a meaningless blanket over the wrongdoing; nothing has been acknowledged. Again, the apology causes a double hurt, because it releases the offender and leaves the hurt in the lap of the other for a second time.

And how meaningful is an apology that issues from an ultimatum, an unattractive choice forced on the other? "Either you apologize, or you will no longer see the grandchildren." There are also peripheral apologies. A person says sorry for various things but fails to address the real source of the hurt. Partial apologies leave an out. They might sound something like this: "I'm sorry if you got hurt. It wasn't my intention to hurt you," or "If I said that, I'm sorry." These statements may provide minor, temporary relief, but they're usually not completely satisfying because in offering them the offender doesn't assume full responsibility for their actions.

So, is the apology effective or is it an apology that causes more hurt? The receiver decides. Being specific about what we're sorry for always increases the potency of an apology (if we haven't missed the mark).

The problem of dual perspectives. Apologies are a muddy business because they always involve two perspectives. Sometimes our own story stands in the way and makes it difficult to apologize for the pain we've caused. For instance, the other says that I didn't do enough to make them feel special on their birthday. I hear how they were hurt by the situation, but something stops me from "feeling into" their pain. I know I am supposed to do the "right thing" and acknowledge it, but is it even humanly possible to fully immerse myself in the pain of the other when my own story begs to be heard? I'm thinking about the efforts I *did* go to, which have not been recognized, or I am thinking about the extenuating circumstances or genuine reasons that made meeting the other's needs difficult. The situation gets confusing, because at what point is telling my own story merely justification and defensiveness? The word *apologetic*, can be described as showing regret, but it can also be about the defense of a position. Why have we come to think of defending a position as a bad thing? Could it not instead be thought of as *one step* in an apology?

Perhaps that's what we don't sufficiently understand—that apologies have various stages. And since they are a matter of the heart, we can't dictate the process. Some of the steps are messy. How many times have you heard, "I'm sorry ... but ..."? Is that a refusal to own responsibility for pain incurred? Or is the "sorry but" an unpleasant glimpse into the apologizer's internal process of weighing what hurt to be accountable for? The actions that follow an apology reveal whether it was a cursory one or the best ever. Heartfelt apologies result in actions that mollify the hurt and rectify the wrong.

Hurt versus offense. Suppose that I can't apologize because though I see the other feels hurt, I don't really see that I've committed an offense. How much integrity would I lose if I admit wrongdoing for something that I don't yet feel guilty about? Would I not then also risk making a sham of apologies? For instance, the other might be hurt by my words or actions, but I didn't say or do them thoughtlessly. Rather, I thought about it long and hard. I said they were abrupt, prickly, or harsh, because the word captured my experience. Can I retract it because the other would feel better if I did? I can't compromise my integrity, and yet since the other remains hurt, that needs to be addressed.

On the other hand, it's possible I don't believe that I've done anything wrong because I can't help but be deceived. We know that the mind selects certain information while overlooking other bits—and deleting some altogether. It could be my mind is working to see me only in the best light; from where I stand, my response is completely understandable. To arrive at an authentic apology from me might require both of us to explore what offense was committed. I might also need to look deeper into myself than I usually do to see my contribution to the offense.

A dicey business. Even if you see that you've done something wrong, apologizing can still be a dicey business. What if because of your apology the other person sits there smugly, thinking that now they're off the hook, and they no longer look for their contribution to the conflict? Apologizing is difficult because it's a unilateral move, where you take responsibility for a hurtful action independently of whether the other person does. Admitting to an offense committed can be humiliating, because it directly affects your sense of self. You've found yourself wanting, and in uttering the apology, you voluntarily incriminate yourself. You might feel that apologizing puts you in a one-down position where you lose face and power. You might feel that you are at risk of being taken advantage of by the other, who has already demonstrated by their behavior that they're not to be trusted. A guideline here: the most important relationship is with yourself. You need to be the person you want to be—and in doing so you might share with the other how scary and difficult it is to be the only one to apologize.

Who apologizes and why. Polarizing around apologies is common. For example, you might say to the other, "I'm always the one to apologize and you never do." If you're the one who apologizes, that might be a good thing or it might not. Why do you do it? How deeply do you feel it, and does it change things going forward? It's possible to get a little holier-than-thou around apologies, harboring the silent belief, "I'm better because I apologize." Or maybe you apologize as a way of backing down, and you do it chronically, hoping to create peace. Perhaps progress or success this time would be *not* to apologize but to hold your ground.

The matter of timing. The timing of apologies can be a perplexing phenomenon to observe. You're thinking about apologizing, but can't quite yet. Or you're holding out for an apology, and the other isn't ready to offer one. In a perfect world you might say, "Let's apologize and move on," but something restrains you—your pride or stubbornness, for example. At other times, though you can't pin down what exactly prevents you, your reticence to apologize feels as if it's attached to something other than your own issue.

As a witness to dialogues during which apologies are granted and withheld, I have come to respect that the timing of apologies holds truths that we can't always see. For example, I watch a wife who can't yet forgive her husband, or a child who's not ready to forgive a parent. Only as I work further with the offending individual do I see that for them to go deeply enough within to bring about the necessary change, they're dependent on the other *not* to forgive *yet*. Granting forgiveness prematurely would cut short the process, and the sustainable benefit would be lost. Of course, such sentiments can only be whispered, because they could be used to legitimize a lack of forgiveness, and an unwillingness to forgive might also come from an unhealthy, stuck place.

Soft and unstable ground. Apologies declared are like putting a stake in soft, unstable ground. Apologies temper matters between the two of you and momentarily stop the escalation, creating an opportunity for your relationship to head in a different direction. But the ground is unstable, because it can give way rather easily. Two people's apologies are rarely perfectly synchronized. What if one acts first—makes themselves vulnerable— and the other either doesn't receive it, takes one more jab, or flatly rejects the apology? Your relationship is still tender and raw, and the softening can easily turn hard and self-protective again, leading to yet another vicious cycle.

Testing an apology. What is the apology test? Remember that hurt has been incurred, trust broken, and the relationship fractured. Even if an apology is meaningful, genuine, specific, heartfelt, and complete, the wall that has arisen between you won't collapse immediately. The person hurt looks for evidence that it's safe to openly trust again. Words of remorse have been uttered, and the hurt one looks for the action that will substantiate the words. Another test of the apology is the willingness to make restitution and repair the damage. The ultimate proof of an apology is acting differently. Failure to change behavior after an apology adds insult to injury. It mocks the process of contrition and causes resentment and bitterness.

Liberating powers. A good apology liberates. Admitting that we were wrong gives us the concurrent experience of being at fault and being appreciated by others. People have a surprising capacity for forgiveness, particularly when the perpetrator acknowledges the impact of their behavior. Declaring a personal failure creates the opportunity for self-forgiveness, self-correction and self-development—learning to like ourselves more rather than using the situation to practice some self-punishing method of balancing the scales. A good apology also results in a better relationship, characterized by more trust and intimacy, because barriers have been removed. Also, when we get our blunder out there, we are no longer weighed down by it and we travel lighter.

When a heartfelt apology isn't forthcoming. There are several things you can do when you don't get the apology you crave. Here is a sampling:

- Keep being who you want to be instead of making yourself dependent on the other's response.

- Grant time to see if the other can catch up. Whether with you or someone else, they might need a few more encounters before they really understand their hurtful impact on others.

- Live in the light of what you know to be true about the other person. Ultimately a person's behavior, not their words, informs the degree to which you either can be vulnerable or need to protect yourself.

- If the other continues to be willfully hurtful despite constructive feedback, then you must make decisions about your own safekeeping, which will naturally inform the future of your relationship.

In this chapter we've examined what you can expect as you re-engage the other in the hopes of interacting differently. Slippage is inevitable, repetition is necessary, and healthy pressure needs to be applied. Getting back on track with the other is approached cautiously, as you look for evidence that gives you reason to trust. Apologies are not always straightforward and yet you need them to re-establish the connection. Your most important relationship is with yourself, because that gives your relationship with the other its best chance.

In Chapter 21, we'll discuss conflict as the intimate connector. This is a bookend to the first chapter, "Conflict—the Great Attractor." We are nearing the end of the conflict journey.

So, What Now?

Since moving through conflict successfully is filled with challenges and setbacks, be realistic about what you can expect from yourself and the other. Making one small change is enough, because it helps you make the next change. Try the following:

- Accept that slippage is inevitable and concentrate on getting back on track.

- Be kind to yourself and the other, because breaking old patterns requires numerous repetitions.

- Know that simply by holding firm in your new stance, you exert healthy pressure on the other.

- Ensure that your apologies are heartfelt, specific, and hit the mark by addressing the actual hurt or harm. Make restitution where you can and act differently going forward.

CHAPTER 21

Conflict—the Intimate Connector

Conflict is a hugely intimate act, which may be why we shy away from it. For as much as we like the sound of the word *intimacy*, how well do we put it into action? Love songs romanticize notions of what it is to know and be known by another. We happily hum their tunes because they reflect our yearning for closeness. We sometimes too freely and quickly label someone a soul mate because we want one so badly. We deceive ourselves into believing that we want or have intimacy, yet it remains a frustrated desire, since many of us don't excel at it, because the idea of having intimacy is different than the reality of being intimate. Could the underlying reason we avoid conflict be about averting intimacy, and might our struggle with intimacy be our fear of conflict?

How do we increase intimate connection? Self-differentiation helps. That's a big word and an even bigger concept, but this is the path we've taken on this conflict journey (more on this below). The crisis of conflict helps us increase our levels of self-differentiation, and the more differentiated we are, the greater our capacity for conflict will be. There is a direct correlation between the two. The conflict road, well-traveled, results in intimate connection. We'll now explore this process in greater detail by first examining self-differentiation concepts as they relate to conflict, and then applying to them three typical relationship problems. We'll conclude by examining what to expect along the conflict road to increased intimacy. But first, let's consider the notion of intimacy and its connection to conflict a little further.

Our Shifty Relationship with Intimacy

Reflect on how much you withhold in relationship, particularly when you know that what you must say will cause discomfort. At times, withholding might be appropriate: the conditions aren't ripe, the motivation is wrong, what we have to say isn't constructive, or we want to preserve legitimate privacy. Other times, we withhold because we've given in to fear and want to evade a difficult situation. Sometimes we don't want to bother with the potential grief that sharing freely could bring us.

At the start of a relationship, we're caught up in our sameness and resonance with the other. How often have you heard it said, "He's just like me"? When we interact without constraint, the relationship feels intimate, and it is—to a point. It feels intimate because the other is generously accepting what we put out there. But perhaps the true test of intimacy is sharing something precisely when we are uncertain of how the other will receive it, or when we know that it will be hard for them to accept the information.

The "shrinking pie" is one hazard in a long-term relationship. In a new relationship, where infatuation thrives, we have the sensation of being fully ourselves because no baggage stands in our way. The fascination is so intoxicating that we think we love the other person, when maybe we're in love with ourselves (or with the feeling of desire). Giving fuller expression to these dimensions of who we are just feels so good. But over time, when infatuation fades and the other gives us a negative response to what we think and want, we start bringing less of ourselves to the relationship. We keep in our thoughts, wants, musings, and so on, or take them elsewhere, and the relationship loses its vitality. The pie shrinks for each of us. However, avoiding the potential for conflict costs us the deep connection we crave.

People readily admit, "I avoid conflict." Reframe the statement to, "I avoid intimacy," and that admission no longer flows off the tongue so easily, because though intimacy sometimes confounds us, we still long for it.

What Is Self-Differentiation?

Self-differentiation is the ability to balance the forces of separateness and togetherness. You focus on both the self and the other, functioning both independently and interdependently. Self-differentiation is the ability to hold on to yourself, to what you think and what is important to you, while still being appropriately connected to the other, whose experience is quite different from your own. You open to feel the tugging influence of the significant other, while you experience the freedom to stand separately and alone, being fully yourself. Differentiation is holding the tension of being *in* what's happening while not being swallowed up by it; being involved and at the same time detached; being connected and separate. (For more information on this topic, see David Schnarch's *Passionate Marriage*.)

Differentiated people are comfortable with their sense of themselves, which is why we've focused on dealing with and embracing the unwanted self. Since such individuals are less inclined to feel that their sense of identity is being threatened, they don't have a desperate need to protect themselves. In short, self-differentiated people are less reactive.

You may have heard someone say, "I have to leave this relationship to be myself." That might be individuation, but it isn't differentiation, the test of which is to be yourself when you're with the other, who is different from you, without the need to make them the same as you. (You still may choose to leave the relationship, but that will be for reasons other than "I can't be myself.")

The Interplay between Self-Differentiation and Conflict
Think about a current conflict between you and the other. In this section, your challenge is to use that conflict to increase your level of self-differentiation. If you can, then you'll also have increased your capacity to do conflict well.

Low levels of differentiation increase unhealthy conflict. Being insufficiently differentiated feeds conflict, as you lean on the other in ways that result in unhealthy entanglement. When you're too dependent, you overvalue sameness because agreement shores up a sense of self, and differences are experienced as a threat. Differentiation requires you to stand on your own. If it was good for you last night, does it have to be good for the other too, or can you abide the differences? What if the real problem in conflict is not *too much* difference, but not enough? Understandably, we blur differences because of our fear of conflict and our inability to stand confidently on our own, but capitalizing on sameness doesn't work because eventually the time-limited, pseudo sense of intimacy is revealed to be a veneer.

Sometimes our fear of the other's reaction destabilizes our sense of self. We fear their lashing out or silent brooding. This then freezes us in a place of low differentiation where we can't freely be who we are. A sobering, humbling reality is that in intimate relationships, we gravitate unconsciously to someone who operates at similar levels of differentiation to ourselves. If we think the other is not grown up or solid enough in their sense of self, then there is a good chance that we aren't, (or weren't) either. Fortunately, we can evolve.

Conflict increases levels of self-differentiation. Perhaps your situation is one in which the difference between you and the other is palpable, and the stakes are high. You can't rely on the other because they're part of the problem. This forces you to a solitary place where you must rely overly on yourself. Conflict sharpens the difference between you and invites you to demand of yourself:

- What do I think? What do I want? Why?

- What's important to me? What am I unwilling to live with?

- How am I the same and how am I different from the other?

When you can't afford to give in on a matter, you step up, and your sense of self is further strengthened. The result is that you become more intimate with you.

Increased differentiation for one increases healthy conflict. As you become more confident, more freely yourself, the other may feel threatened and disoriented, because you don't need them in the same way. Propelled by fear, they attempt to reinstate the old dynamic between you. Unconsciously or consciously, they poke at your areas of self-doubt, with the hope of subverting your new direction to diminish their own anxiety. They might get you to question your thinking, the wisdom of your intended actions, how you'll impact others, and what this says about you. If you give in to self-doubt, you get more of the same between you and the other, and your level of differentiation does not increase.

If you keep pressing to do things differently, the other must step up in a way they haven't previously. They feel the pressure and are forced to decide.

They can fight your change, which means the two of you will likely enter a tug-of-war where, for a time, it feels like you're both losing. Alternatively, the other could see the train leaving, run like fury, and hop on the caboose before it pulls away from the station.

As one of you reaches for increased self-differentiation, conflict escalates. Then you might be tempted to be less of yourself, simply for external peace (though not necessarily for internal peace). But when you sell out yourself for ease in conflict, being intimately and emotionally connected is impossible. The dilemma is that being yourself causes conflict, and not being yourself creates distance between you, and more internal conflict, while the forces of connectedness and separateness play themselves out. But the amplified fight caused by increased differentiation is necessary and healthy.

The role of self-differentiation in the change process. How does change happen if being differentiated means "I can be me and let you be you"? How can you just let the other be, if the current issue impacts you directly and negatively? Differentiation can't simply mean backing down, particularly when the issue matters to you. Surely that would be the easy way out, at least in the short term. This is the moment to be autonomous, hold your ground, and declare yourself. You aren't telling the other they must change. You are simply being clear on what you can and can't live with. You deal respectfully with the other and the relationship by sharing what you need to operate successfully into the future. (Each of you lives in the full knowledge that all decisions, change and no change, result in consequences.) Rather than simply remaining silent, you create opportunity for adjustments to be made, thereby safeguarding relational health into the future.

Four Signs of Being Self-Differentiated

Signs are helpful because they confirm that you're on track and point you in a direction. One of the benefits of being differentiated is that the quality of your relationships substantially improves.

Regulating your own emotion. You develop the ability to self-regulate when your emotions make you uncomfortable. (Self-soothing is one of the first skills we try to teach our young, and as adults, we're often still honing that skill.) When you aren't getting what you need from the other or you're feeling threatened, you find a way to take charge of your emotional state.

Also in a self-differentiated state, you're less affected by the emotions of the other because you recognize them, and the other, as separate from you. This is particularly important when the other attacks, blames, or belittles you. You see that this is what they do when their emotions have control. Inserting a thicker filter between you and the other at this point is vital, because otherwise you'll likely absorb their emotion, passing it back and forth between you. Next time just observe what happens to the anger, fear, or anxiety. Do you both end up wearing the emotion, or does one offload it and the other pick it up? Self-regulating takes place in this challenging context.

Using two brains simultaneously. A sign of being differentiated amid conflict is the ability to access and maintain your cognitive functioning during heightened negative emotion. As you have traveled this conflict journey and increased your understanding of what is going on inside you, you have also been training your neocortex to resume its executive function and manage your limbic system. When the two brains work together, distinguishing your stuff from the other's becomes easier, as does being more autonomous and using empathy in viewing the other.

Contracting appropriately permeable boundaries. Being self-differentiated affords you greater wisdom in determining how permeable or impermeable the boundaries between you and the other should be. Losing yourself in relationship occurs when the boundary is too permeable, which grants the other too much influence over you. On the other hand, impermeable boundaries, possibly caused by fear or an inflated self-concept, wall off the other's influence, as does believing that you're right and don't need others. Imperviousness can cause as many problems as letting too much in.

The degree of permeability is context specific. Imagine an adjustable dotted line encircling you. When the external influence is too costly, the spaces between the dots should be tight, and when outside influence would be helpful, the spaces can get loose. You allow yourself to be influenced without being driven by external forces. You depend on input without becoming overly dependent on it. Failure to find a healthy balance destabilizes you. The permeable boundary both separates from and connects you to the other.

Gaining respect: the handsome dividend of differentiation. Even if the other doesn't agree with you, you garner respect from them simply because of the way you conduct yourself. In a differentiated state you are clear, quietly confident, and compelling. You set reasonable limits and at the same time are empathetic and respectful. With finesse, you communicate how you see things, what is important to you, and why. You do this without putting the other down in the process.

Three Relationship Scenarios

In each of the three scenarios that follow, differentiation helps you get through. As you reflect on the situations, think about the person closest to you with whom you're experiencing conflict, whether a spouse, long-term partner, colleague, family member, or friend.

In a mood. The other is depressed, anxious, grumpy, angry, sad, fearful, and so on. What impact does their state of mind have on you? Does their mood bleed into yours and change how you're feeling? Do you erect a barricade so that you aren't affected by their mood?

In regards to the other's mood, what is a self-differentiated response? You let yourself feel the pervading presence of their state and decide how much you can afford to let in. You recall all that you already know about this mood and the role it plays in your relationship. You look at its history, its function, your response, and its impact on you over time. What does all that tell you about what you need to do now?

Third party trouble. Your other is having a problem with a mutual friend, workmate, or family member. Where do you position yourself in relation to the two parties? How do you manage yourself amid their conflict? How affected are you by what your significant other thinks, and how do you act on what you think?

When your partner is at odds with your mother, for example, self-differentiation helps you find a way. You can't afford to deny your partner's experience (without massive consequences on the home front) and hopefully you also want to be supportive. Yet you're in a dilemma because your experience of the third party is different, and your partner's fight isn't yours. Perhaps you respectfully hold your separate positions rather than blurring them, because that's what is real for you, and meanwhile you support your partner with all the sensitivity, care, and heartfelt empathy that emanates from another soul who also knows pain. Otherwise your partner could feel betrayed by you when they need you most. You can be the healing witness who comes alongside without being in the same mental, emotional place as your partner. They don't even need you to feel the same way they do (sometimes that comes as a surprise). You determine how permeable the boundary needs to be to allow your partner's experience in, while still holding on to your distinct experience.

Painfully different. Your other has a significantly different view of something that really matters to you, and you want your views to be the same. The issue may be one of values; you hold dear family Sundays and your partner feels enslaved by the obligatory dinners. Perhaps your beliefs vary significantly; you believe that children need considerable freedom to explore and learn from their mistakes, and your spouse believes that they need strict outer controls to learn inner control. Or perhaps your physical desires vary in a way that is costly to you; physical affection is your love-language and your spouse doesn't put a high premium on relating physically. The difference eats away at you and the tensions between you rise.

In such situations, self-differentiation is put to the test. The difference between you is painful because the other doesn't deliver what you need. You're at their mercy because you haven't yet found a way to meet your own needs. When the other can't or won't give you what you need, you have no one else to turn to but to yourself. (You may still declare what you are and aren't willing to live with, as is described above.) If you refuse to look at yourself, you have no recourse but to escalate the conflict by blaming the other for not being there for you in the way you need. This situation requires you to take a braver stand than you have previously and strengthen your capacity for separateness.

Remaining differentiated is perhaps a direction to commit to rather than a goal to attain. The reality is that we move in and out of differentiation, depending on the situation and seasons of our life. The greater the stakes, the greater our investment, and the greater our interconnectedness with the other on a matter, the more torn up we might feel. We will feel the tugging influence of the other while we feel an opposite pull within. Yet we know that we can't afford to let go of either—and that this, too, shall bear fruit.

Along the Conflict Path toward Intimacy

Finding a healthy balance between separateness and togetherness can feel like sitting on a teeter-totter—the weight constantly shifts. In a long-term relationship, often one person repeatedly puts weight on either separateness or togetherness, whichever is opposite to the other. That in itself creates conflict, and since a fight is propelled by an unmet need, doing conflict badly feels as compelling as doing it well. You are moving either toward or away from intimacy. But deciphering healthy separation from unhealthy distancing gets muddy, because the process usually happens in gray zones, not in black and white. When you're fortunate to get a good outcome, healthy separation leads to greater intimacy with yourself and with the other. But if you don't get the latter, at least you end up with greater intimacy with yourself. Standing alone while declaring yourself helps you know and understand yourself more. Unhealthy distancing, however, maintains the conflict. Here are some realities you will encounter on the path toward intimacy:

- You will feel discomfort regardless of the direction you travel. If you are moving toward unhealthy distance—away from intimacy—the gap between you will work you up inside. If, with the goal of greater intimacy, you are moving toward healthy separation—standing your ground and being a fuller you—this new territory will still feel uncomfortable, and the other will likely poke at your self-doubt.

- The process is rarely straightforward. You might make headway toward more intimacy, get tripped up by yourself or the other, and turn back toward unhealthy distance, falling prey to old habits. The back-and-forth fuels the conflict between you.

- You feel the need to distance from the other, yet you are bound together. As though symbiotic, you need each other to take the next healthy step. You couldn't do it on your own. For instance, Phaedra determines that she can no longer afford to succumb to her spouse's insecurity. That forces her to wrestle through her own self-doubt, find her voice, and take the necessary action. This then forces her husband to step up, soothe his own insecurities, and adopt new action. The interactions between them are the fertile ground for change and growth.

- Choosing not to be more intimate with yourself results in unhealthy distancing, and the conflict between you and the other remains. There's a good chance that if you have a reactive need for more distance from the other, you're distant from yourself (although at times you determine that distance from the other is the healthy option because of who they have shown themselves to be; but you decide that with a clear head).

- Conflict affords you an efficient way to get to know the other more intimately. You're offered a rare glimpse of the raw material that constitutes their inner makeup. Though what is revealed might not be attractive, still you get to see what's important to them, what they're willing to fight for, who they become in stressful times, what they can't afford to compromise on, what happens when they're backed against a wall, and where goodness triumphs or fails.

If you can remain open to the needs of the other and simultaneously hold your own needs, a healthy rebalancing can occur.

Let's consider three challenges to intimacy aroused by conflict:

- The irony is that to be intimately connected, you must be willing first to be disconnected from the other.

- You must whisper the squirming truth *of* yourself *to* yourself. Speaking that truth to the other is an even greater challenge. Confronting yourself out loud, in the presence of the other, increases your vulnerability and consequently the intimacy between you.

- You must let go the outcome of conflict and focus instead on who you are in the process. That's the best way to achieve increased intimacy as opposed to the distance normally associated with conflict.

Tipping the Scales toward Intimacy with the Other

When you are caught in another vexing interaction, remember the following:

- To increase your chances for intimacy, fight like there's going to be a tomorrow. Allow the possibility of a continuing relationship to affect what you say and do, and limit the amount of damage you inflict.

- Recognize that your put-downs range from covert to blatant. They might be so subtle that even you aren't aware of what's in your heart until you utter them, or until the other sees the pattern and finally calls you on it. Put-downs, disrespect, and blaming increase defensiveness in the other and therefore detract from intimacy.

- When you see an interaction going sideways, arrest the damage by changing the context. Sometimes a fight poisons a physical space and moving to a new venue can be helpful. Sometimes you need to take a breather so that you can re-engage differently. Take a longer bathroom break and have a good look in the mirror before leaving the sacred space. The combination of a break, a breather, and a change in venue provides the opportunity for fresh beginnings.

- Rather than latching on to the other's fault, flip it around and see the positive side of the same characteristic.

- Rather than holding out for agreement with the other, create some good traction by respectfully communicating to them your understanding of their perspective. Watch for de-escalation of the negative emotion and a shrinking gap between you.

- Use the gift of humor to lighten and build as opposed to taking a shot and destroying. Laughing at yourself is a good place to start: "Ah, I can't believe I said that. I'm so full of it."

- Conduct yourself with grace, despite the other's behavior, because that is your best chance at creating intimacy. Remove the reason for them to fight with you and let the other fight with themselves.

- Know that there are some people you will choose never to be intimate with, because you believe them when they show you who they really are.

As you value your differences and intimacy grows, you and the other experience mutuality— not in a needy way, but by recognizing that the other makes you better. As you nurture independence and interdependence, you bring a fuller self back into the relationship, and the shrinking pie becomes an expanding one. You see that you are *more* individually—and together—than either of you are on your own. The vulnerability each of you has experienced and witnessed amid conflict connects you more profoundly and results in a renewed vitality in your relationship.

So, What Now?

The conflict journey takes you down a path on which you get to know yourself and the other more intimately than ever before. Conflict increases your ability to be self-differentiated—holding on to yourself while remaining connected to the other—and the more differentiated you are, the greater your capacity for conflict will be. Try the following:

- Be prepared for pushback from the other when you stand alone and declare your position.

- Find constructive ways to soothe yourself, particularly when you feel threatened or deprived of what you need from the other.

- Determine what kind of a boundary is healthy between you and the other. If you lose yourself in relationship, then you're likely allowing the other to have too much sway over you. On the other hand, if you don't allow the other to influence you, then likely your boundary is too solid and you might be missing some valuable input.

- Enjoy the benefits of staying the course in the conflict journey: a more peaceful, developed sense of self, and a more vital, connected, and intimate relationship.

Conclusion:
Let Conflict Change You

How interesting it would be if we all spoke together about what we have gleaned from the inevitable conflict in our lives! I have learned so much and have been challenged to use my identity struggles to transforming ends while I work alongside others who courageously engage with relationship discord. In these concluding pages, I'll share several themes that stand out for me as I reflect on the transforming journey through conflict.

Using Conflict to See

We look, but do we see? I once had a dream that I was going about my life as usual, preoccupied with something that seemed legitimately consuming, and off to the side on a park bench was an older woman. When I took note of her, she looked up at me with a penetrating, yet gentle and impassioned gaze and said three words: "Don't you see?" They were so important to me that, in the dream, I tried to record them. I wanted to retain the words and share them with others.

The older, wiser one inside us all, the one who sits to one side and witnesses our life, calls out to us, "Don't you see?"

Don't you see what's happening? "I'm looking but I can't see—I'm not sure what I'm looking for."

Don't you see what you keep doing, repeatedly? "I don't feel like I have much choice, although there must be options."

Don't you see what's really going on for you? "I've become disoriented and the truth is obscured."

Don't you see what's really going on for the other? "What I know is that their actions have a potent effect on me, and they've got me scrambling."

Don't you see their antics for what they really are? "Just when I think I see it, the other manages to confuse me and I lose my clarity."

Don't you see that there could be another way? "If I could, I'd be going that way, O Wise One!"

One step back, our older, wiser self has a view that's lost on us when we are ensnared in conflict. The older, wiser one within sees what we don't see.

Noticing what we need to see takes a really long time. We know this because, thus far, we have been unable to end the pain. We've been stumped by our own internal barriers, and the significant others in our lives have also done their part to maintain those blocks. At certain times, helplessness isn't just an out; rather, it's a legitimate reflection of the hopeless context in which we find ourselves (environment *does* matter), or the wiser self within doesn't always show up, and hence we miss what we need to see.

Conflict reveals to us that something must change, but we need to help each other, because it's hard to find a better way. Sometimes, we're drowning, about to go down without a lifeline, and though we are surrounded by people, we have effectively camouflaged the outward signs of our desperate inner struggle. Other times, if we have eyes to see, ears to hear, and the courage to take action, we'll throw the lifeline to someone else. Perhaps, as we depend on each other, we'll come to recognize what's needed to wrest us out of the craziness of our life and do things differently.

Letting the Tension Work for Us

Tensions between us and the other fuel those within, and those within fuel those between. If we can hold the tension, change has a chance.

Tension seems to be programmed into our biological and relational makeup. For example, becoming autonomous is fraught with difficulty. Parents and teenagers will be at cross-purposes at least some of the time, and when young adults don't appear to give sufficient thought to consequences, a parent's fears are activated. In any close relationship, particularly with a spouse, polarizing around individual differences is a natural response to tension. One is a spendthrift and the other a tightwad. One partner is nourished by touch while the other appears oblivious to its absence. Being out of sync with each other's needs creates the tugging tension, both within and between, and perhaps the restless balance.

Tension is an integral part of our lives, and maybe that is just as it should be, because tension has a magical quality. It cries for resolution. We listen to a piece of music and wait expectantly for the chord that will bring resolution, or the transition that will shift the mood. If we don't hear the resolution, we might hum it audibly or silently. When we're reading a book, we imagine what will happen next, anticipate the way out of a predicament, and speculate about how it's going to end. We engage the scenes and fill in the blanks. We gravitate to relationships that do something to us. While we hold tension, important changes take place within.

We discover the best and worst of us in stressful times. We examine our fears and decide which ones we need and which we can let go. We see what form love takes, when it rises and when it falls. When we experience painful individual differences, we might reach a level of understanding that produces mutual shifting toward each other.

Discovering the Value of Questions

Critical to increasing self-awareness, reflecting is made possible by questions. Questions invite the kind of introspection that's just unsettling enough to nurture ongoing change. One reason conflict is so distressing is that it raises disturbing questions about us, to which there are no simple or comfortable answers. When the other wrests us from a homeostatic state, we silence questions to calm the inner turbulence and get the other off our back. We settle for fabricated answers when they aren't really answers at all. Even very smart people are satisfied with familiar non-answers, because an oft repeated though insubstantial response temporarily pushes aside an unnerving question. When the question returns, however, we recognize that we're still stuck.

A fight holds hope for change because to get through it we must revisit our answer or remain at an impasse. (Over time, the other can't settle with our answer either.) What is the deeper explanation or more critical question that resides just beyond where you usually halt? The very nature of questions is to unsettle, revisit, and broaden a perspective. They function to open up instead of close down. Inquiry is the antidote to apathy.

Questions keep us mulling over a situation. It's like they merge the wide-angle and zoom lenses, simultaneously expanding the field and homing in on detail. Questions pull at the edges, revealing what has been forgotten, hidden, or neglected. Questions invite input from less worn ways of thinking, and ruffle sacred assumptions. They feed imagination, possibility, and humor. Questions also lead to provisional answers; we know just enough for today. We hang on to the answers revealed, but not too tightly. Let the questions do their work. Let them open us to our inner conflict, inch us forward, illuminate our way, and reveal rich worlds begging to be explored.

Feeling What We Don't Want to Feel

Over a lengthy career of helping people navigate conflict, I have concluded that, though we frequently experience intense emotion, we're not very good at identifying what we feel, and our emotional vocabulary is elementary at best. We're familiar with the word *anger*, might get stuck in it, but struggle to attach to it a more nuanced description. The primary emotions that make us feel vulnerable are the ones we have particular difficulty naming. If we pay attention to our emotion longer, we improve at describing it, discovering what's causing it, and deciding what to do about it.

My brother once told me that he thinks of feelings like waves. They build, crest, and then dissipate as they reach the shore. Feelings need to be honored because they inform us of what's important. When we address the vulnerability behind a defensive feeling—the specific hurt or fear behind anger, for instance—we reach the heart of the matter. Just as every wave vanishes at the shore, intense emotions don't go on forever. They dissolve into new experience.

I have been encouraged by how even the most miserable feelings don't last—*and* they can carry us forward. The beauty of the shore is the solid ground. My daughter once said to me, "I don't think you love me. I haven't felt loved—I think you love [one of her sibling's] more." As a mother, I felt dreadful and experienced immense inner conflict. How had I missed the mark so badly? I had failed to give my daughter what I valued the most. Had a spirit of judgment and confusing standards of right and wrong blocked the flow? I was at a complete loss about how best to deal with the tensions between my children. Each of my thoughts was more disturbing than the last. For three days, waves of sadness, anxiety, guilt and regret grew, before they finally crested and began to dissipate—and as they did, the thoughts I noticed surprised me: "I have failed. I got it wrong …"—and the next part came slowly—"and maybe that's okay." Then entered lighter, more calming thoughts like, "Part of the human condition is to fail and that's how we connect most soulfully with each other." These emotions opened me to fully hearing my daughter's pain and to taking every action to meet her needs now. If we can feel what we don't want to experience about ourselves, we will find a way through it to a freer place.

If we can come alongside the other when they're feeling what they don't want to feel about themselves, a potent healing moment is created. The power of empathy made a lasting impression on me when two of my daughters, who were very young at the time, were fighting with each other, and one came to complain about the other. I was trying to buy myself some time because I didn't know how to deal with the situation and said something like, "Oh that's terrible. You must be so sad." She twirled in her frilly skirt and skipped out of the kitchen. Empathy was enough for her. Feelings are physical sensations that make their own way through our bodies, if only we let them.

Being Patient in Change

I've asked myself if I put too much emphasis on our changing. Clearly, accepting ourselves for who we are must be the first step, and it may be enough. But the question brings up the *why* of change. We pursue personal change for two reasons: we are dissatisfied with ourselves (and our life), or a significant someone is dissatisfied with us.

Still, after all this, the question remains: "Do people really change?" I have been discouraged to see my old patterns emerge long after I thought they were extinguished. I see my behavior's hurtful impact on the other and my role in maintaining a vicious cycle. When the other pinpoints my faults, it resonates within. I would like to see change in myself … and yet. Real change is so hard to come by.

What is the real impetus for change? Do we change because we independently want personal transformation, to be a better person? Perhaps we get tired, eventually, of behavior that shows us who we really are and prevents us from being what we want to be. However, in my experience, change that is solely driven internally is reserved for the unusually motivated and hardy few.

Often, the other serves as a catalyst for change, which is interesting because partners will often say to each other, "Don't change for me. Change for you." Evidently, as much as we'd like to say we change for ourselves, we're more dependent on exterior incentives to push us along than we'd like to admit. Perhaps it's more accurate to say that we change *because* of the other. The most important people to us help us just by being who they are. When our behavior is no longer tolerated, we must find a new way. When we're in a dilemma where no option is acceptable, we reach out uncertainly and creatively for change. A cost that is too high, such as losing the other, serves as an impetus for change.

Even though I'm in the business of change, working with this material has given me fresh eyes, a deeper understanding, and even respect, strangely enough, for why people don't change. We are caught up in an intricate, resilient web, both internally and externally. Many forces hold limitations in place, and we're brilliant at taking the edge off the discomfort a limitation creates. In addition, we readily succumb to the ample "outs" available to us:

- *The blaming out*, because the other's behavior gives us legitimate reason to focus on them rather than on ourselves.

- *The passive out*, because tackling the limitation requires too much effort.

- *The comfortable out*, because people come along to support and commiserate with us in times of trouble.

- *The paralyzed out*, because there are just too many uncertainties, and indecision trumps action.

- *The complicated out*, because we are overwhelmed and can't make sense of what's really going on.

While I have developed a deep respect for why people don't change, my belief in the possibility of change has only increased. I find myself encouraged and hopeful. Make a change in one place and it affects change in another. The very nature of change helps us. On this transformative journey, we can allow ourselves to be "done to" by the situation, the other, and the ensuing internal struggle, while fully acknowledging that we're also like tumbleweed rolling wildly in the wind. There's no straightforward path to our destination.

What if fifty percent of people changed because of their conflict with the other? That would be an encouraging number. What if we let seventy percent of the hurtful things we experience wash over us and found opportunities for growth in the remaining thirty percent? That would also be a good number. What if we decided to engage in one experience a week, a month, a season, or a year for personal change? What effect would that have over a lifetime? Those are some statistics worth thinking about.

Let's be patient with ourselves and others, and let's notice the subtle shifts in our thinking, or simply the directional change of our action. Life is merciful, so we have many chances to choose something small, something manageable, in the timing that works for us.

Not Needing Perfection

It would be wonderful if all fractured relationships were eventually reconciled, if looking back, the pain of conflict always seemed worthwhile and we unfailingly arrived at a better place, together. But sometimes that's not what we get and relational strife remains. But if we can produce fruit from the pain of our struggle, then the journey has not been futile.

Perhaps we now see something about ourselves that alters our view of others. Maybe we more effortlessly extend compassion or forgiveness. Based on what we've learned, we might change destructive patterns going forward. As dreadful as the hurtful experiences were, perhaps as our hearts broke wide open they also expanded, enabling us to love more extravagantly than ever before. Our relationship to pain is only useless if we walk away empty-handed.

Struggle and beauty are so intricately bound together that disentangling them is often impossible. What do we do with our pain? It needs to be acknowledged and honored, but what then? Pain needs to be redeemed. I have come to believe that by converting our pain into a unique contribution, we can make a considerable difference in the world. After all, we understand our pain intimately from the inside out. Because of our experience, we have a vested interest in the issue that causes us pain. When we hear about someone in similar circumstances, we can build a bridge to them and empathy flows. That is energy to be harnessed for good.

Perhaps we can come to value all human relationships, even be grateful for them over time:

- For the frustrating ones that have kept us up at night, outstripped our regular coping mechanisms, and left us at a loss about what to do next—because they have helped us understand ourselves more.

- For the upended ones that hold a dull pain, where there has been no reconciliation—because they remind us of a broken world, a complicated reality, and complex humanity. They fill us with humility and fuel our need for one another.

- For the ones that have miraculously turned around—where real, tense, challenging encounters have been the stepping stones to deep, nourishing relationships—because they fill our soul with hope and warmth, foster our belief in humanity, and let us rest in life's unfolding.

Conflict is a crucible for transformation. It pushes us toward our fears and sensitivities and at the same time affords us an escape from those same fears. When a sore spot is activated, if we courageously tend to the pain, we create an opportunity for healing. When we face the unwanted self, if we transform by exceeding our limitations and moving closer to who we want to be, then the pain has not been useless. When self-doubt threatens to shut us down, if we wrestle through the fear, we realize we're capable of more than we knew, and as we look back, we recognize self-doubt as our growing edge.

Nothing is perfect … and yet the imperfect world feels like a warmer place. I find myself thinking, "It's alright … It's really alright." I'm welling up with a deep-down, quiet happiness that overflows and becomes compassion for others. I'm resting easier, traveling lighter, laughing more, and loving better. I'm grateful for the fight, because it brought me here.

CPSIA information can be obtained
at www.ICGtesting.com
Printed in the USA
BVOW08s1634270118
506475BV00002B/259/P